Other Books by Donna Hartley

Fire Up Your Life!

Fire Up Your Intuition!

Healing restores the body, mind, and soul

To Sheba,
my loyal Himalayan cat
who taught me when you love,
healing happens.

To Angela,
your wisdom and guidance
was insightful,
you are a saint.

Fire Up Your Healing!

A Journey to Restore
Relationships and Health

Donna Hartley

AUTHORITY
PUBLISHING

Fire Up Your Healing: A Journey to Restore Relationships and Health
By Donna Hartley

1. Body, Mind & Spirit : Spirituality - General 2. Body, Mind & Spirit : Healing - General 3. Biography & Autobiography : Personal Memoirs

ISBN: 978-1-935953-44-9

Cover design by Lewis Agrell

Printed in the United States of America

Authority Publishing
11230 Gold Express Dr. #310-413
Gold River, CA 95670
800-877-1097
www.AuthorityPublishing.com

Remarkable, Astonishing, Informative, Inspirational...

Fire Up Series

In these uncertain times, the human spirit yearns for hope and enlightenment so each of us may survive and thrive. The **Fire Up** series recounts a compelling true-life journey, delivering timely inspiration along with timeless wisdom. Donna Hartley is crowned Miss Hawaii and her attention is captured by a kind and patient soul, George, who mysteriously prophesies that her success is paved with learning lessons. He relates to her in storytelling form that Donna must survive three life-threatening events if she is to fulfill her destiny. Is George a wise man, a mentor, an angel, or all three?

Fire Up Your Life! recounts Donna's near-death experience in a DC-10 plane crash at Los Angeles International Airport, which occurs directly after she expresses her desire to change her life or die. Trapped in the flaming inferno, she receives a mysterious message questioning her actions on Earth. She wills herself to survive and is the last passenger out of her section of the aircraft. With the steadfast help of her teacher, George, the reluctant student Donna begins a journey of spiritual transformation, committing herself to change her fearful and unhealthy lifestyle. Her first assignment is to fight for improved airline safety regulations. Next she must conquer her destructive relationships with men. Moreover, to become a successful entrepreneur, she must master her fears.

Fire Up Your Intuition! finds Donna distraught in an emotional and financial crisis. George unexpectedly appears and bestows on her five mysterious envelopes that hold a 30-day assignment that he calls "the gift of intuition." The banter and discussion continue between student and teacher as Donna works to acquire insight into her own intuitive awareness. Her faithful Himalayan cat, Sheba, is by her side as Donna follows George's program step-by-step to learn to trust her feelings and act upon them to master *the knowing.* George predicts that when she completes her assignment, her dream to adopt a daughter will come true.

Fire Up Your Healing! narrates the sometimes rocky path on the passage toward family forgiveness leading to emotional maturity and the strength to heal. Life-changing events alter her path as a set of "coincidences" guide her to her destiny. Donna travels from the tragic confines of her mother's post-stroke nursing home to the somber quarters of the judge empowered with deciding the fate for the bitter court battle in which her stepmother has embroiled Donna and her brother upon their father's death.

George, her master teacher, adamantly advises her to release her anger in order to survive. Could she forgive the alcoholism, the violence, and the indifference? This skill is now essential if she is to survive her stage III melanoma. Could she develop a "perfect plan" in order to raise her six-year-old daughter? Would her 35 lessons learned carry her through her darkest hours? George mystically appears in the hospital to give Donna a shot of spiritual adrenalin and the courage to face down the deadly disease.

Fire Up Your Heart! begins at the gravesite of her stepdad as a heartbroken Donna deals with the eleventh death of family and friends in the past few years. Her nagging intuition forces her to consult a heart specialist and the prognosis is her worst fear: she must have immediate open-heart surgery to replace her failing aortic valve. Mariah, her daughter, now age ten, is the driving force to help her live. Donna's friends rally to lend her support for the delicate surgery scheduled for **March 1st**, the same date of her plane crash and melanoma diagnosis. What are those chances? Donna must summon all her strength and hard-won wisdom to survive. Will George spiritually guide her through this life-threatening operation? Has Donna learned her lessons so she can cheat death for the third time?

Contents

PART III
WHAT, MORE HEALING!

Acknowledgements

To Stephanie Chandler, my publisher, whose expertise and creative process helped navigate me through the complexities of a four-book series. You are a wealth of knowledge.

To Amberly Finarelli, my editor at Authority Publishing, who is gifted with the professional talent for grammar and punctuation. You are a master editor.

To Jeanne Snoza, my confidant, who encouraged me to write the soul-searching truth about healing.

To Jacki Willette, whose calming effect and computer savvy saved my sanity during the completion of these pages.

To Sue Kass, my girlfriend, walking partner, and strawberry-jam-making buddy, who made me laugh dozens of times when I wanted to give up.

Part I

Let the Healing Begin

Flashback

"Tighten your seat belt! Tighten your seat belt!" a flight attendant shouts.

"Head between your knees…grab your ankles! Head between your knees…grab your ankles!" another attendant yells.

I'm going to die in this inferno. As I bent down to grab my ankles, I could see the flames rising above the window from the left wing of the plane. The aircraft was hurtling off the end of the runway with a load of passengers and a belly filled with explosive fuel. My body shuddered as my mind comprehended the reality that there was no way out of this burning aircraft. *No! No! I have to heal with my mother, father, brother. This plane does not have the right to take my life.*

My career in Los Angeles as a would-be actress is failing miserably; suicide has been my dominating thought. My only hope is that this trip will change everything as I head back to the Hawaiian Islands as a former Miss Hawaii to emcee the upcoming pageant. Change! I want change…but not a plane crash.

A flight attendant screams, "Come to the rear!" Smoke assaults my lungs, and savage flames engulf the entire rear exit of the DC-10 cabin as

I fight my way to the back of the plane, colliding against bodies whose only mission is to flee before the aircraft explodes and seals them inside. Suddenly, I stare mesmerized at a wall of flames, inches from the exit door, understanding my escape is blocked. In a matter of seconds, my perceived reality shatters, when the near-death experience alters how I understand my existence. An all-encompassing calm descends upon me, with a rush of euphoria and a sensation of profound tranquility. Time ceases to be. My quest for understanding is born, and my spiritual journey ignites as I encounter a white filtered light and a perceived inner voice resonates within me.

Have you spent your life
complaining or creating?

Again the calming inner voice questions me.

Do you love yourself?
Do you have a good relationship
with your family and friends?
Are you living your goals and dreams?
If you die today, have you left this
planet a better place for being here?
"No!" I need more time... I want to live!

In mere seconds, my life is altered. How could it not? In the past I had not played by life's rules; I wanted to do it my way. But now the universe insists I obey a higher calling.

Besieged by the smell of singed human flesh, passion ignites in my soul as I vow to live my life differently. Step by agonizing step, I navigate myself through the blinding smoke and menacing flames to the exit door, fighting for my life!

Chapter One

Why Is Healing So Painful?

My body shuddered as I shook my head, forcing myself back to the present. Glancing around at the aircraft's confined interior; the plane was still sitting on the tarmac waiting to take off. For me, airplanes are like the bell to a dog in the Pavlov experiments. When the bell rings, the dog is conditioned to salivate, trained to expect food. Every time I board an aircraft, the fear of the unknown accelerates my heart rate. I always flash back to surviving that fiery airplane accident on take-off at the Los Angeles International Airport, twenty years ago.

The reality was, right this second, I was on the runway at the Reno-Tahoe Airport. *I have to rid myself of fear. Learn to live in the now. I can't let my past dictate my future.*

Yesterday I received the news that my eighty-two-year-old mother had suffered a debilitating stroke and was in Intensive Care in a Pennsylvania hospital. There were so many unresolved issues with my mother. My mom, an Irish fireball who divorced my father in the 50s, went against the norm because she was determined that her children would not starve. She filed for separation when I was in the hospital at six with malnutrition. The outcome of the bitter divorce was she carried her unresolved anger with her and later it turned to drinking.

Could this plane deliver me in time to say the words I yearned to say before she passed? I clutched my chest as I thought that I might arrive too late. Slouching in my seat, I stared at the subdued interior ceiling of the plane, with deep breaths in an attempt to calm myself.

The flight from coast to coast took the entire day and I fidgeted in my seat, wanting to be there already. A day was hardly enough time to release years' worth of disappointment I harbored over my mother's and my relationship. At least this flight was allowing me some time for soul searching and to prepare what I wanted to say to my mother. My mentor, George, had insisted I would heal with my mother. Would we heal before she died?

A small voice filtered through my thoughts. "Mommy? Mommy?" Then louder, "MOMMY!"

I jolted upright, turned my attention to the seat beside me where my daughter sat. Mariah's little hand reached over and touched mine. "Mommy, I love you."

I had waited a lifetime to hear those words from someone who really meant them. I couldn't help but wonder how a four-year-old would know the right words at this time. I studied my little brunette. She leaned in closer as I set aside my concerns about my dying mother. Mariah needed my attention. At the last minute and with Labor Day almost here, I hadn't been able to find anyone to look after my daughter. Plus, I didn't know how long I would be back east. I also thought if John, my stepdad, could see his granddaughter, it might distract him from some of the stress he felt about his wife's condition.

"Mommy," she asked softly, "is Nana going to die?"

Tears welled up as I struggled to speak. "I don't know. I'm praying for Nana to stay alive, but if God wants her in heaven, then she'll have to go."

"That will make me sad," Mariah said while twisting her little fingers.

"Me too, but it's okay to have sad feelings." Sensing a need to change the subject, I picked up her Winnie the Pooh book. "How about I read?"

"Oh, yes. Pooh Bear! Read to me."

After the second reading, Mariah spent time poring over the pictures, all the while making little comments. I smiled as her little voice rose an octave. "You funny bear, Pooh. You love to eat honey. Honey, honey, and more honey!" My animated little daughter was so much like me; she loved to talk.

My mind slowly drifted back to my gravely ill mother. The big question: would I make it in time? Then I admonished myself. *Don't think like that! I'll make it in time. I'll see my mother. I will heal with her.*

I closed my eyes to rest, but my mind reverted to when I was six and hospitalized due to malnutrition. My father traveled and did not leave money with his wife. In fact, that is why I ended up in the hospital, no food. While I lay in the hospital, fighting for my life, my mother filed for divorce. She was adamant her children would not starve. As a battered woman, she flew with me and my brother in the middle of the night.

The financial burden of being a single mom of two children in the 50s was overwhelming. My mother and father continued to despise each other after the divorce, making me and my brother pawns. They never spoke a word to one another after the divorce became final, so my brother and I would have to communicate the insulting messages they said about one another from one parent to the other. Christmas and other holidays were hell—one parent would be extremely upset because my brother and I chose to spend the day with the other. We paid for it with verbal abuse and emotional manipulation for months to follow.

I had choked back anger and resentment toward my mother for more than thirty years. She didn't approve of me being an actress, she didn't consider it a real job—even when I entered a career as a professional speaker, she insisted it was a joke. The issue she harped on the most was that I couldn't get or keep a man. Bottom line, according to her, I was too picky. The vicious divorce battle, and later her disease of alcoholism, altered our relationship. The drinking accelerated before I left for college. So many nights I cried myself to sleep, praying she would stop.

But nothing cut deeper than my mother's refusal to acknowledge my adopted daughter. It amazed me that after eleven attempts to adopt, and seven years of waiting, she couldn't support my decision to become a single mom. Sure I had wanted the whole package with the husband and white picket fence, but it didn't happen. I decided to move forward; adoption as a single woman was my path. Mariah was a beautiful baby with little pink hands and toes, and plenty of energy. On her first Christmas, a package arrived from my mother addressed to Mariah. She didn't hold it against Mariah being born, only my decision to adopt. That was my mother's style, stay upset with me but not take it out on the innocent child. The despair that swept over me was abandonment— Mariah had a grandmother, but I didn't have a mother. My mom wouldn't even talk to me the first year of my daughter's life. When Mariah turned two, my stepdad insisted that I come home with his granddaughter for his seventieth birthday. It was a strained visit, but Mariah was such a happy-go-lucky child she warmed my mother's heart, even if our words were guarded. We never discussed that we didn't speak for two years; it was buried under the carpet. Forget and move on.

Now, in my fifties and having a daughter myself, I understood that I always loved my mother and I do believe she loved me. *I should have shown more appreciation for everything she sacrificed for me. Did I understand what she had endured? Her pain?*

Suddenly, my mentor, George's, words came to me clearly, as though he were alive and sitting in the seat behind me.

Let go of the past
Live in the present

Mariah tugged on my sleeve and in a cheery tone asked, "How long, Mommy?"

Checking my watch, I said, "Only an hour. I am going to drop you off at a babysitter while I visit Nana. "

"I want to see Nana," her little voice stated with authority.

Reaching over, I held my daughter's hand. "Sorry, you can't come to the hospital. I'll tell Nana you sent her a big—and I mean an enormous—

hug with lots of kisses too." I smothered Mariah with kisses.

My little daughter giggled and her eyes sparkled as she snuggled by putting her head on my lap. What a gift, a blessing, Mariah was in my life... *Hold on, Mom. I'll be there soon.*

When the aircraft landed in my hometown of Bethlehem, I felt relieved. My girlfriend picked me up and volunteered to watch Mariah while I went to visit my mom. The next hour passed in a haze until the taxi stopped in front of Saint Luke's Hospital. I thrust a handful of bills at the driver, jumped out, and ran into the bustling lobby. Anxiety seized my stomach as I scanned the registry and found the Intensive Care Unit was located in another wing.

By the time I reached the nurses' station, my heart was pounding and my nerves were stretched tight as a drum. I clutched the counter, announcing breathlessly to a petite woman dressed in greens, "I'm Donna Hartley, here to see my mother, Catherine Klopack. Is she...?" Words stopped coming from my mouth. I couldn't speak because I didn't want to think it.

Love your family
Love yourself too

The nurse looked up politely, as though she had seen hundreds of family members like me before. "You can go in and visit. She is in the room directly behind you."

Turning quickly, I glanced though the Intensive Care room's window and saw my stepdad, John, a strikingly handsome man, standing by her bed. He looked like he had aged ten years since I had last seen him. I considered John to be my real daddy and always felt closer to him than my father.

John greeted me with a hug, holding on tightly. His ironed, white shirt was crisp against my cheek, and the pens in his breast pocket clinked against each other. His shoulders stooped and I could sense his sadness. Emotionally overwhelmed, I struggled not to cry. "I'm glad you made it," he said. "Your mom is putting up a terrific fight and I know it will do her a world of good to see you." His voice grew thick. "We came so close to losing her. But you know your mother, one stubborn woman with a will of iron." He let me go and cast a long and loving look at his wife where she lay in the bed, hooked up to all kinds of machines.

"Look, Catherine," John said softly, his face a stoic mask, even though my mother's eyes were closed. "Donna is here, your daughter." He choked with emotion as he said, "I'll give you two a few minutes alone. Don't worry, Catherine, I will be close by. You're doing great." He leaned in closer to my mother's face and tenderly continued, "You'll be back to your old self in no time."

He whispered to me so my mother couldn't hear, "Be in the cafeteria. Talk to your mother so she won't be frightened."

I gazed down at the frail, pasty-looking woman before me, scanning her arms, looking for somewhere that wasn't taped, pinched, or pierced; a place that I could touch. Three fingers on her right hand were free of wires. Very gently, I began to stroke them, but there was no acknowledgement that she even knew I was there. I missed seeing the sparkle in her eyes, as her eyelids remained shut. Her auburn hair was matted, her round face with a few freckles appeared sunken and lifeless, and her five-foot-two frame seemed to have shrunk. She was a powerhouse of oomph, but not now. She looked so old. A single tear trickled down my cheek. "Mom? Mom, it's me, Donna. Mom, I'm here." I stared at her but there was still no reaction. "I love you. I do. I'm sorry we didn't communicate more."

You spend energy putting up armor
to protect yourself
Then a lifetime ripping it down
so you can heal

Unexpectedly, her eyes shot wide open with a look of terror as the machines in the room reacted with alarm buzzers and loud beeps. She opened her mouth, struggling to speak, but nothing intelligible came out. A nurse rushed in, pushing me aside. After examining my mom closely, she reset the monitors. Seeing the fright on my face, she explained that this is a common occurrence with stroke patients. I didn't understand what she meant; all I knew was that my mother was calmer now and that was good. Her eyes were closed again.

A chill; I shuddered as an unsettling sensation surrounded my thoughts, that this woman of monumental stamina might die any minute. Though she had been hospitalized for a week after being severely beaten by my father during the divorce battle, she fought to recover her health and had to scrub floors to put food on the table for her children. To purchase a small house, she took all of her jewelry and laid it down in front of the builder as a down payment. He was so impressed with her determination he hired her on the spot to sell more of his newly built homes.

Were the difficulties of her life too great? Did the numbing of alcohol block it all out? Why didn't I understand this before?

For years I blamed our strained relationship on myself, believing that I was somehow flawed and unable to meet her standards. My mother wasn't the type of person who gave complements or said "I love you." She harped on my weight. I had to be slender if I wanted a husband. I tried to overcompensate by staying slim, courtesy of bulimia. I earned a college degree by selling pots and pans door-to-door and being awarded every major honor the company offered. I even won the prestigious title of Miss Hawaii. At twenty-five, I moved to Los Angeles to pursue an acting career, which my mother insisted I was wasting good years of my life on a foolish dream.

The plane crash abruptly altered my path and propelled me to leave the Hollywood lifestyle behind and move to Lake Tahoe. At the age of thirty-two, I became a mountain gal working as a cocktail waitress for the first time and trying to understand why I survived the plane accident. What was my real purpose in this life? By delving into my spiritual journey, I came to realize my childhood issues would always taint my accomplishments. Understanding the nature of the problems didn't mean I was emotionally equipped to endure them. I still had lots of baggage when it came to my family. I had never felt I fit in, always like the outsider. Our family never talked about issues, just covered them up. Now, looking down at my mother, for the first time faced with contemplating her mortality, I thought, *What do I do with this knowledge now? How do I heal my past? Can I forgive and forget?*

Hearing someone behind me, I turned to see a man dressed in a blue coat. He stated he was the attending physician, but what he said was hazy because I was caught up in my thoughts. Finally I responded, "I'm her daughter, Donna." Quickly I continued, "What are my mother's chances?"

His sympathetic pale blue eyes gazed at me. "Every day she's alive she gets stronger. Her chances are better. We'll know more after the next couple of days. I do need a few minutes alone with my patient now, if you don't mind."

As I left the room, I immediately began searching for my stepdad but saw no sign of him. It was time to speak to my brother in California. We had both been informed when Mom was taken to the hospital. We had talked a half dozen times as I confirmed my plans to fly home to Bethlehem immediately and agreed to call Doug and update him on our mother's condition.

After the first ring, Doug picked up.

"I'm here at the hospital with Mom," I anxiously blurted out.

Without saying hello, he said, "How is she?"

I steeled myself to be the bearer of bad news. "Brother, it's not good. The stroke has paralyzed her. She can't move. She can't talk." My voice quivered as I continued, "She's hooked up to all sorts of machines."

"Wait, have to turn down the music," Doug said, his usually gruff voice soft with concern. "What does her doctor think?"

"He said we should know more over the next few days." I sighed. "I believe she could hear me talking to her, but it broke my heart to see her lying there so helplessly. Even if she lives, what kind of life will she have? Maybe with time and therapy..." I didn't finish my sentence. In all fairness, I had to be realistic with Doug. "At her age, it'll take a miracle. Two packs of cigarettes and twenty drinks a day. It's amazing she made it to her eighties."

"Is she going to die?"

"I don't know," my voice trembled. "Let me tell you, Brother, there is nothing you could do this Labor Day weekend that is more important than coming to see her. I think you need to be here. Soon!"

There was silence. Knowing my brother, the rational and organized one in the family, unlike me, the emotional drama type, he was weighing the pros and cons. Should he wait until there was more information from her doctor? Could he be away from his business at this time? He finally said, "Let me coordinate some details at the office. I'll start making arrangements." There was a long pause again. "I'll get back to you when I have my flight schedule." My brother was not the type to express his emotions, very similar to our biological father in that respect.

Would my brother arrive in time or be too late to say goodbye?

My mentor's words raced through my mind.

Heal now
Heal later
Heal at death
Heal after death
You must heal

Lesson Learned:

Healing starts with you

Chapter Two

Listen to Your Heart

The next few days were a blur. Sitting in the Intensive Care Unit, emotionally drained, I gave myself a pep talk every day—no, more like every hour. Here I was an inspirational speaker, yet I was lacking in hope. *I must be strong for my mother. I must be positive.*

Possibilities of what could happen to her bombarded my brain. The days were long and tedious, with only the intermittent company of the vigilant staff of nurses and doctors. I couldn't help but wonder what the long-term prognosis would be. Would our prayers to mend her damaged body work?

My personal struggle was leaving my daughter with a babysitter from early in the morning 'til after dinner. By the time I picked her up, I was exhausted and didn't even want to hear what games she played or read her a nighttime story.

During the drive back to my childhood home, I did my best to reassure Mariah that she was being a great kid and I loved her. We both climbed into my childhood bed, and Mariah begged me to read her storybooks and I only yearned for sleep.

Every day at daybreak, Mariah quietly slipped out of bed and went down the stairs to greet her grandpa at the kitchen table. When he drove home late at night after leaving his wife at the hospital, John stopped at the local corner store. He would surprise Mariah with chocolate donuts or chocolate milk, or even chocolate pudding. They chatted away as she devoured her sugar fix. When I greeted them at the kitchen table, it was the only time on this visit I saw my stepdad laugh or smile. I shook my head over the appalling breakfast. John only grinned. Then he would kiss his granddaughter as she giggled before he headed to work. After he finished his day, he drove directly to the hospital to sit with Catherine.

Each morning I steeled myself as I walked into my mother's hospital room and saw little change in her condition. Every so often her eyes would open and focus on me intensely. The veins beneath her skin looked like thin blue ropes and her face was a road map of deep lines. Because the stroke had stolen her voice, I would spend hours recounting old adventures to my mother. Today, forcing myself to set my worries aside, I began with stories about our dogs.

Inching my chair closer to her, I began, "Did I ever tell you how much I loved growing up with our dogs?" I kept filling in the silence as my mother stared at me. "Remember the two Chow Chow dogs we had when I was in high school? The male, Shang Wong, whom I called Shangy, was supposed to be Doug's dog, but he bonded to me. I loved his champagne color and his unique purple tongue. He protected me." I chuckled asking, "Did we have those big dogs so when the high school boys came around they were forced to behave?" I smiled down at her. "Now that I'm remembering it, I think there was a method to your madness. Yep, sorry, Mom, didn't give you enough credit." I chuckled again. "I recall my dates saying they didn't like my dogs. If a guy tried to put his arm around me, Shang Wong came charging in the room and stopped right in front of him. I thought he was a cuddly ball of fur, all 65 pounds of him, but my date didn't!"

She seemed to be watching me intently, so I continued, "Quacky, our duck, now that was some house pet. I don't think he knew he was a duck.

Got him for Easter when I was five, right? Then Doug's buddy accidentally broke the poor animal's leg. Hysterical, is what I would say to describe my reaction. You insisted that I calm down as you filled the bath tub with water and a big rock at each end. Quacky swam back and forth while quacking all day long. When his leg healed he was sure of his status in the family and would follow me everywhere, even to the school bus. I was so embarrassed. More like mortified. That was one sociable duck."

My mom's eyes fluttered and finally closed. Leaning back in my chair, I listened to her labored breathing. My feelings were raw as I wondered what the future held for the woman I had cherished when I was a young child.

About an hour later, I continued my dialogue. "Did you ever know how much I loved living in Hawaii? Hanging out on the beaches was the best. Oh, that's right, I convinced you I should go there because the University of Hawaii was international. Trust me, I did go to all my classes. Well, most of them anyway. Thank heavens I learned to sell pots and pans door-to-door to earn a scholarship. Mom, I became good at selling. Maybe I inherited that from you. Well, selling isn't the exact word, more like I learned survival skills. At first I hated hawking cookware and thought it was beneath me, but in the long run it was my ticket to freedom. Yep, money to buy a sports car, travel to Europe, pay for my apartment, and yes, I had the latest surfboards. The surfing bug bit me when I lived there."

Mom struggled desperately to speak, but only gurgling noises emanated from her mouth. Her eyes flashed with panic and distress. I stroked her fingers. "It's all right. It takes time. Your body had a shock. You will recover." I said it with such conviction that I almost believed it.

After a few minutes, it appeared that she had fallen asleep again as I watched her closely. Now it was my mother's time to fight to live. Had I gleaned survival skills and determination from her? I reflected; I was my mother's daughter, whether or not I wanted to admit it. I had inherited her fair Irish skin that reddened in the sun before it turned to even a hint of tan. Freckles; I had those too. Our hair was the same shade of red, or was hers more auburn than mine? Our hands were our main form of expression when we talked. You would have thought we had Italian blood, but not at all. We both had our compulsive behaviors to fight. I had been bulimic, binge eating and then throwing up. My obsessive behavior manifested itself 180 degrees in the opposite direction of my mother's. She drank; I ate and threw up.

When a nurse entered the room to check my mother's vitals, I was startled. The stern- faced woman nodded and reassured me that my mother could hear and understand what I was saying. She insisted that I should keep talking because it was therapeutic and would help in her recovery. She must have seen me through the glass window chattering on hour after hour with my one-way dialogue.

Moving around the room as the nurse checked my mother's stats, I gawked at the machines, wondering if Mom would be hooked up to them for as long as she lived. *Why didn't we have more fun together? Why didn't it occurred to me that we should have been more patient with each other?*

After the nurse left, I got myself a cup of hot black tea to soothe my hoarse voice and ramp up my energy to continue the monologue, praying this could help my mother remember and assist in her regaining her strength. This time I focused on my daughter. "You'd be impressed with your granddaughter, she has quite the vocabulary, or maybe I should say she never shuts up. After she wears me out, I tell her to chat with the cat, and after that I tell her to talk to her goldfish. Her only complaint is that Sheba and the fish can't answer her questions."

John arrived after work. He always stayed with his wife until he was sure she was comfortable and asleep for the night. I kissed him and left to collect Mariah from the babysitter. Though my girlfriend had generously helped to take of Mariah, after a few days, I decided I wanted Mariah to be with other kids her age, so I contacted another friend of mine, whose daughter had two children of her own and was home every day with them. Kim was petite, round, and full of energy.

As soon as I entered Kim's house, she pulled me aside with a somber look on her face and said, "Donna, I need to tell you that Mariah's been missing you something awful. She constantly asks for you and seems pretty upset. I know she's worried about her grandmother, but I think she's concerned about you too."

"What do you mean?" I questioned.

"She keeps asking when you're coming to pick her up. It's more than just a mere question. She thinks you'll die. She's afraid of being without you."

As if on cue, Mariah came pouncing into the room and I swept her up in my arms. Handing me her drawing, she announced, "Mommy, Mommy, look what I drew. It's Grandpa, Nana, you, me, and Sheba! Isn't Sheba cute?"

Holding up the picture, I inspected it. "You're becoming a wonderful artist! I love it. Thank you so much." As I marveled over her stick figures in different colors, Mariah beamed.

Unexpectedly, she grabbed the picture, scrambled down, and started running back to the living room while shouting over her shoulder, "Forgot to color the grass! Be right back." She stopped, turned around, and lunged back at me throwing her arms around my waist. "Mommy, I'm glad you're here."

The realization that I was away from my daughter from 8 AM until 7 PM each day sparked my emotions. What were her fears? She was only three, and even though she kept up a constant stream of chatter, she didn't yet have the words to describe the complexity of her feelings. Hell, I didn't even understand my own confused emotions. Mostly I felt guilty about dividing my time between Mom and Mariah. Torn between the two people I felt responsible for. Should I continue to spend the day with Mom or break it up to be with Mariah more? *What should I do? But my mother needs me more, doesn't she?* An unsettling feeling kept nagging at me.

The journey is about
trusting your feelings

I pulled into the driveway. The white split level home with brown shutters surrounded by old maple trees and an expansive lawn brought back a rush of emotion and nostalgia.

After I moved away from home, how could I have taken so many left turns when I should have gone right? An answer came to mind. *Because I had to do it my way.* I cursed under my breath. *Too late now to go back and change my choices.*

While tucking Mariah into my old bed, I told her that Nana was slowly getting better. We read two books, or I should say I read the books while she marveled over the pictures and added her own interpretations. This procedure was very time intensive, but finally she fell asleep with the last book on her chest. A quick fix, but hopefully she could sleep with the knowledge that her world wasn't crumbling. Even if it was.

As I tucked the blanket around Mariah, she abruptly woke up. I stroked her forehead and sang soft lullabies while glancing around my bedroom, at the desk and knickknacks collecting dust on my dresser. Mariah rolled over on her side, put her little hands under her head, and drifted back to sleep. Kissing her goodnight, I whispered, "Sweet dreams, little Miss Tulip." That's what her Grandpa called her.

Getting ready for bed, my brain would not shut down. Staring into the mirror while brushing my teeth, my anxiety level accelerated. Speaking to the distraught figure in the mirror, I asked, "What should I do? Answer me now." To keep me and Mariah sane, a decision had to be made. When should we return home to Tahoe? Doug would arrive the following day. Should I stay or leave? If I left, would my mother understand that I was not abandoning her? If I stayed, would Mariah feel I was neglecting her? Back and forth I went until the wee hours of morning.

Decisions empower you
to take action

I climbed out of bed weak-kneed and lightheaded as if I were coming down with something; had I eaten much lately? It was still dark outside, with no sounds of movement on the street. My eyes fluttered as I murmured, "Make a decision." Standing in the center of my bedroom, appreciating it was still decorated as I had left it when I headed off to college, a flood of memories overtook my psyche as I glanced at my trophies I had won as a ski racer, ribbons from dog shows, and my well-worn black rocking chair.

Mother's condition had stabilized and she would be moved out of Intensive Care within a few days. With my brother's impending arrival, tomorrow night, Mariah and I could return home to recharge ourselves and spend some time together. I thought about my mother and worried that she still needed me to be with her. Or did I need her? I sat down to meditate or at least attempt to center myself.

Within a few minutes, a quick flash surged through my mind. *Go home to Tahoe.* I had learned from my mentor, George, to take action when I felt an intuitive insight. Without hesitation, I called the airlines and booked our return flight for the next afternoon.

Would Mom recover? Would I heal with her? What if I didn't?

Lesson Learned:

Learn from your past

.

Chapter Three

The Voice from Within

My brother spent twelve days in Bethlehem helping with insurance and locating a full-skilled nursing home for our mother. Doug and John agreed on a facility and asked for my input on the phone. I was relieved Mom could be moved out of the hospital. Brother and I spoke every day, and after Mother was transferred to the twenty-four-hour care facility, he felt he could consider coming home to California. He filled me in on the facts, letting me know there was little change in our mother's condition, but emotionally he didn't reveal much.

The responsibility of managing my speaking business, raising a young energetic daughter, and worrying over what was happening back in Pennsylvania, I was plagued by insomnia.

This night was no different; I tossed and turned, with my comforter ending up scrunched   at the bottom of my bed. In and around my home you could hear a pin drop, but I couldn't seem to shut down the noise in my mind. Near midnight, I finally dozed off into a half-conscious state that mimicked sleep.

At exactly 3:10 AM, my eyes shot open, focusing on the digital clock across from my bed. I sat straight up. My heart pumped wildly inside my chest and my scalp tingled with apprehension. A lightening-like flash exploded inside my head. My hands, of their own accord, pressed against the sides of my face as I heard: *You must be with your mother on Tuesday.*

I had been meditating for more than 25 years—sometimes more faithfully than others. The more I meditated, the more I experienced messages that echoed in my consciousness. At first I brushed them off as unsubstantiated feelings, but certain seemingly coincidental occurrences in the past taught me to pay attention, and to take action. Hadn't my mentor, George, come to Lake Tahoe six years ago to teach me the five levels of intuition with those envelopes of mysterious instructions? Hadn't I learned to trust my intuition? Now was the time to honor my gut feeling, because my thinking wasn't totally rational. *Tuesday. Tuesday. You must be with your mother on Tuesday. Oh my God, Tuesday.*

This was not the first time I had experienced impromptu flashes of information that demanded my full attention. They came and went in mere seconds, but the messages were insightful. George had insisted that I meditate daily and trust my intuition. In fact, during the last year of his life, he devoted much of his time to working with me to understand the gift. I was a stubborn student, but he never gave up. Over the years I learned to respect and rely on my visionary flashes, attributing my survival of the plane crash and the decision to adopt my daughter to my intuitive insight. George mysteriously sent the smell of his cherry pipe tobacco to the hospital hallway when I was adopting my newborn daughter. Even though he had passed on, George was there in spirit.

What an amazing man, who answered my hundreds of questions. I argued with him, wanting to know if there was an easier path in life. One of the last times I saw him, he made a point of telling me that my intuition would guide me, especially in times of crisis. Dear, sweet George, a man of wisdom. How I wished he were still here; I could really use a strong shoulder to lean on. He had been there to guide me through some rough patches in life, and now my heart ached for the gentle man who had entered my life in an unusual way.

It was 1970. I had just been crowned Miss Hawaii and was walking off stage when a heavyset gentleman with an Oklahoman accent, smoking a pipe that reeked of cherry tobacco, congratulated me and told me I deserved to win. At first I thought he was weird, but something about him was so kind and familiar that I was drawn to him. George had a unique way of making me feel at ease, as if he understood my soul. Later, when he predicted certain things, I knew he was really different, and when his predictions came true, we became fast friends. George: my wise man, mentor, and now my angel. *Sure hope you're watching over me because I could use some guidance.* Thinking about George reminded me of one of his many pearls of knowledge, which I had dubbed Georgeisms.

**Listen to the voice within
and you'll know the answer**

Tuesday. Oh my God, Tuesday. I threw back the covers and hurried upstairs to my office to check my calendar. I flicked on the overhead lights and focused on the upcoming week. I had a speech on Sunday for a national association, but Monday was clear. I could book a flight for that morning and be back in Pennsylvania for whatever was going to unfold on Tuesday. Afraid that my rational self would talk me out of calling the airline, I immediately picked up the phone and booked two seats. Family, I was astonished at how important my dysfunctional family was to me. I raced downstairs and pulled out the big thick envelope George had given me, called the "gift of intuition."

Family

When you interact with your family, treat them with gentleness, kindness, respect, and love. A loving family environment provides a safe haven where you can belong. It's a place of refuge, where hugs are plentiful, common interests are shared, and feelings are talked through.

When the outside world becomes lonely and fragmented, we turn to our family for comfort, safety, and understanding. We benefit from shared wisdom, resources, and support. If you make a mistake or are harsh, apologize. Keep the lines of communication open. No one is perfect. Sometimes it is difficult, but be forgiving and accepting. Unconditional love and deep bonding are the rare gifts a family can give.

AFFIRMATION:
I love my family

After reading the affirmation a couple of times, I tiptoed into Mariah's room and sat on her bed. I wanted to hold her, to shield her from the disappointments of the world. Picking up her favorite stuffed doll with frayed pink yarn hair and a tattered pink dress, remembering it was given to her by Nana. Tears trickled slowly down my cheeks, and then my crying accelerated until I was near hysteria. I backed away from the bed, afraid I would wake my sleeping daughter.

Suddenly, Sheba, my Himalayan, came careening into the room, meowing as loud as she could. She stared at me, and then at Mariah's bed, as if assessing the situation. Quickly she made a decision and started weaving in and out of my legs while continuing to meow, forcing me to lean down and pet her.

"Sheba, for such a little thing you certainly are perceptive," I said in a soft voice as I gasped for air. Sitting on the floor, I gently stroked her. In reality, she was soothing me.

Gazing over at my daughter's peaceful face, I wondered if she'd understand why I needed to cart her back east again. I prayed she would understand.

Looking back at Sheba, I continued, "Hey, Kiddo, Mariah and I have to leave again. We have to. Something is…" I grabbed my chest. *Mom could die.*

My focus centered on my mother now, infused with turmoil and worry over the woman I was afraid I didn't know. I had been so busy with my life that I hadn't taken the time to understand much about her. Had she lived the life she wanted? Did she feel loved? My nagging inner voice kept saying, *Get sleep! Rest! Prepare!* I didn't know exactly what I should prepare for, but could only hope it wasn't the worst.

Sunday, presenting my "Fire Up Your Life" inspirational presentation was like an out-of-body experience. It was as if I were watching myself speak, and the words flowed effortlessly from my mouth. Whatever I said must have worked, because I received a standing ovation. The presentation came from my soul and bypassed my brain. I wrote the experience off to sheer exhaustion.

Early Monday morning, I walked through the house checking for any last-minute details. Sheba's food was assembled on the kitchen counter for the cat sitter, and I had left on a light. Doors and windows were locked, the suitcases were packed and in the car. Mariah snuggled in her car seat, munching on her favorite cereal from a baggie while waiting for me. I glanced down at Sheba, who was staring at me resentfully, and said, "Sorry to leave again. Mariah and I will miss you something terrible." As guilt washed over me, I choked up and mumbled, "Left you special treats!"

While closing the door, I heard the phone ring and quickly fumbled with my keys to reopen it.

"Hi, this is Donna," I declared.

"Glad I caught you," my stepdad stated in a flat tone.

"Is Mom okay? Is something wrong?" I blurted.

"She's fine, but she had to be taken back to St. Luke's Hospital. The doctors want to run more tests." His voice became so faint I could hardly hear him.

"Daddy, what did you say? I couldn't hear you."

He cleared his throat. "She is having trouble breathing."

"Oh, Daddy," I said instinctively, remembering the eye-opening flash that woke me up at 3:10 AM.

"Don't worry; you'll be here in a few hours. I'm so glad you're coming." I could hear the anxiety in his voice. "Catherine is fine, the doctors are being cautious. Have a safe flight. I wanted you to know." His voice trailed off. "Tomorrow we'll see what the doctors have to say."

"Don't you worry either. Be sure to tell Mom I love her and will see her soon. Can she talk at all?"

"Not yet, but she hears well enough. Now, I have to work on Tuesday, so I am grateful that you can spend the day with her. I leave early in the morning. You take your mom's car, drive Mariah to the babysitter, and be at the hospital as soon as you can." John could have said all of this to me when he picked me up at the airport, but he sounded like he needed to review the details to make sure everything would be just right for Catherine.

"Okay, see you at the airport." I wanted to say more, but what could I say? *I had a premonition that it was crucial I be with Mom on Tuesday.*

Nervous and restless during the entire trip, my mind was constantly churning. I wouldn't arrive until near midnight on Monday. *Why do these plane trips take so long?*

Let go and trust

Hurrying through the sterile hospital hallways Tuesday morning, I was afraid of losing Mom, fearing the worst about my premonition. Anxious and unsure of what the day would bring, I entered her room and approached her bed. I heard her labored breathing, her lungs wheezing, and saw her face was drained of color. Her stroke had frozen the left side of her body and impaired her right.

Pulling up a wooden chair, I sat down, still desperately needing to heal with my mother but struggling for words. Regardless of her ability to respond, I had to let her know that I loved her unconditionally. *Would my daughter someday do the same thing to me, be hurt and withhold her love?* Suddenly it was all so clear; this was my lesson, to finally let go of the pain of the past and forgive us both for the years of anguish. I was determined to break the negative patterns and not repeat the cycle of miscommunication with my child. I wanted to be there for my daughter.

Love is unconditional
Love is forgiving

It was an extremely long day of battling my emotions, attempting to be strong for my mother as I watched her expend effort just to breathe. *Our egos... She had to be right. I had to be right. I had to do it my way no matter what she said.*

It was 6 PM and nothing had happened. The day passed without incident and I began to wonder if my intuition had been clouded by lack of sleep and worry. The message was clear... *You must be with your mother on Tuesday.* Perhaps I had assumed the worst. Was I needed at my mother's bedside because her husband had to work? Was that all it was?

I gazed down at Mom, studying her. She appeared calm, although her breathing was still labored. I decided it was safe to leave and pick up Mariah, knowing that John would be here within an hour. Turning to pick up my sweater, I heard it—a blood curdling sound. My mother's chest heaved suddenly and her eyes flew open in terror as she attempted to gulp in more air. Fear framed her face, frozen in an open-mouth gape.

Grabbing the call button, I pushed it repeatedly with all the strength I had. Her desperate gasps permeated the room as she struggled to breathe. "Help! Someone! Help!" I screamed.

Two nurses ran into the room and a third nurse followed with a fully equipped crash cart and a doctor who barked at me to step aside. I stumbled back from the bed. The medical staff surrounded Mom, obscuring my view, but nothing blocked the horrible sound of her death rattle.

"Her airway is blocked and she needs a tracheotomy. It's a straightforward procedure; do we have your consent to proceed? We have to do it now," the doctor insisted.

"She signed a living will. She does not want life support procedures! A copy is on file. You must have it." Panic gripped me. I couldn't move. I felt a terrible constricting pain in my chest. A grim thought. *Oh, no. What if it's at the nursing home?*

"Are you the decision maker?"

"No. Her husband is."

"A family member can make the decision and it must be made now," he said adamantly.

What do I do? What should I do? "Phone! I have to call my dad!"

A nurse rushed me to the main desk. Hysteria spiked my adrenaline and my hands were shaking as I pressed the numbers.

Pick up! Please pick up!

"Get my dad, John," I shouted to the man who answered the phone at the club where John had been president for the last forty-some years.

John came on the line and said breathlessly, "What is it, Donna? I was just on my way to the hospital. Is Catherine...?"

I interrupted him by speaking louder. "Daddy, you have to make a decision! She needs a tracheotomy. You have to say yes or no right now!"

"Calm down. What is happening?"

"Mom can't breathe. The doctor said she needs an emergency tracheotomy! I told him she has a living will and wouldn't want this."

"No operation! I'm on my way." I stood there listening to the dial tone for a few moments.

I turned and ran back into my mother's room. "Her husband is on the way. Fifteen minutes," I shouted to the doctor. "You have to wait!" My mother looked dreadful, with a pasty color to her face as she gasped loudly, struggling to suck in air. "She has a living will. A copy should be in her records. Please someone find it," I begged.

The doctor looked at me sternly over his glasses. "I don't think she has fifteen minutes."

Lesson Learned:

Trust your intuition

Chapter Four

It's Still Tuesday

Mom shouldn't die like this, battling for every breath. She deserved to pass peacefully with grace and dignity, surrounded by those who loved her, not in a room full of strangers waiting to cut a hole in her throat. It wasn't supposed to be like this.

I moved to the end of the bed. *Dear God. Please help her. Please,* I begged.

An oxygen mask was placed over Mother's nose, but she became frantic and somehow found the strength to raise her good hand up and rip it off. As soon as the nurse replaced the mask, my mother yanked it off again. Another nurse injected a sedative into her IV, with the intention it would quiet her.

A sickening emotion slowly washed over me as I sensed a negative feeling that charged the room. *Is this what death feels like?* My hand flew to my chest, sensing an oppressive, heavy feeling in the air. Was it death's grasp or something more sinister? The room grew colder. I sensed a shadowy cloud levitating over my mother. I blinked several times, convincing myself this was a figment of my imagination. Was this apparition a form that transported the spirit away?

Catherine desperately struggled between life and death. Her eyes fluttered open with a look of horror, then abruptly closed and then opened again with her head shaking. The bank of monitors affirmed she was alive as they beeped wildly. I felt a sudden overwhelming sense of negative, black energy surrounding her. My intuitive inner voice abruptly exploded in my brain. *Leave my mother alone!*

Immediately I called in God's protection. I surrounded her with love. My intent was completely focused, and in my mind, only my mother and I were in that room; even the doctor and nurses were invisible to me. *I love you! I love you! I love you!*

Slowly my mother started relaxing, although her body still jerked. Her breathing was irregular, but her gasping sounds softened. I could feel the negative energy dissipating from the room. All of a sudden, her eyes focused on me like a laser beam, and a moment passed between us where I understood she was not going to die today. Did she feel that as well?

How could I understand what happened? What was it? Was my imagination playing tricks on me because I was afraid? Placing my head in my hands, I tried to make sense of what I had experienced. *Tuesday. It is still Tuesday. I had to be with my mother on Tuesday.*

Even when nothing makes sense trust your gut feeling

"What's going on? What's wrong with Catherine?" John blurted out as he hurried into the room.

I looked at him, too bewildered to say anything.

The doctor took him aside, saying, "Your wife was having difficulty breathing. She was Code Blue. We thought we might lose her. Her breathing has become more regular in only the last few minutes, but she still needs watching."

Quickly, a tall nurse walked into the room, announcing, "Here's the living will."

The will, the freaking will. What took so long?

I smiled slightly at John and said, "Thank God you're here. Mom is a lot better now, but she had me scared."

He glanced over at Catherine and then turned his gaze on me. His voice quivered. "I should have been here with her, but thankfully you were," he said, giving my hand a gentle squeeze.

"Please tell me I did the right thing. I know she doesn't want any life-saving measures, but they couldn't find anything in her records. They kept pressuring me to let them proceed and warning me that we couldn't wait for you." I struggled to speak as I felt overcome with emotions. "The doc...the doctor said she might not make it."

He gently wrapped his strong arms around me and said, "I'm so sorry you had to go through this alone, but you did exactly the right thing."

You must be with your mother on Tuesday. I collapsed into a chair as John sat near the bedside of his wife. He insisted he would stay the night and promised to call me if anything happened. He suggested I pick up Mariah and get some rest. Emotionally and physically drained, I gathered my things and kissed them both good night.

Stopping at the hospital room doorway, I glanced back at John, standing next to his wife, and then at my mother lying lifeless in the hospital bed. She was ashen, and the oxygen mask covered most of her face. I sensed the bond between them. Love. I smiled. Because of what had happened between us in the room just moments before, whatever that was, I felt the time with my mother would be extended. I wasn't sure, but I had an intuitive feeling that this was true. I could heal with her. How it would unfold I had no idea, but the healing had begun.

Lesson Learned:

Act on your intuition

Chapter Five

The Healing Begins

It was the beginning of November and two months had passed since my mother was released from the hospital and transferred back to the nursing home. The stroke had made eating very difficult for her. To eliminate the worry that she might suffocate or choke, John, Doug, and I had consented to a feeding tube being inserted into her stomach. A feeding system wasn't an operation like the tracheotomy. By the terms of her living will, she was able to be kept comfortable with medicine and food. Now she was battling an infection from the feeding tube and John had asked me to fly back and help him make a decision of whether to remove it or not.

It would be a short visit, a few days, to Pennsylvania, and I couldn't take Mariah on another emotional trip. She needed to feel secure in her own surroundings. I hired a nanny, a college grad from New Zealand, who would stay at the house with her.

Walking through Kirkland Village Nursing Home, I noticed a lingering disinfectant smell as I passed the solarium where patients watched television with a vacant gaze in their eyes. A depressing feeling sickened me. John had told me several days ago on the phone that only a few of her friends had stopped by to visit Kitty, as they called her. I know this saddened him.

Where were all her drinking buddies? Catherine had friends who drank with her for twenty–five years. Where were they now? Where was her best girlfriend, Marilyn, whom she drank with and smoked endless cigarettes. They traveled to Florida every winter for a couple of months and my mom paid all the expenses. Mother insisted I should be more like Marilyn, outgoing and the life of the party, fun at the bar. That always annoyed me, since I thought Marilyn was a leech, taking advantage of my mother's generosity to pay for trips and drinks. Where was Miss Life-of- the-Party now?

Continuing down the floral-wallpapered hall to the end where my mom's room was located, I entered and glanced around, noticing all the framed family pictures I had sent. There was a bouquet of red artificial roses on her nightstand and a bird feeder outside her window. John claimed Catherine watched the birds for hours, and he took care of refilling it every week. The same bird feeder had been outside their kitchen window at home, so seeing it here brought some continuity to her life.

Silently, I moved to the side of the adjustable medical bed, and she slowly opened her eyes. *You're pale. You look frail.* The doctors had informed the family that she wouldn't walk again, or even sit up on her own. Her body was unresponsive to physical therapy, but with speech training she would be able to say a few words.

I placed the large plastic bag I was toting onto a chair and cleared my throat to sound cheerful. "Mom! I have missed you so much and I'm here now to tell you I love you." Leaning over, I kissed her a few times.

A flicker of a smile grazed her lips.

A good sign. I opened the bag and beamed. "I know you like nice clothing. Surprise! I bought you some new outfits." I had spoken to her nursing staff a few days before I arrived. Rather than leaving her in pajamas, they suggested that getting her dressed every day would do wonders for her morale. Her hazel eyes seemed intent on watching me, even though one eye drooped. The entire left side of her body remained paralyzed. Only her right hand and arm were capable of limited movement. What did she have to learn from enduring this stroke?

"Let me show you how beautiful you are going to look. Here's a royal blue outfit, with a gorgeous blouse and matching slacks. The color will be wonderful with your hair. Do you like it?" I asked as I turned the set from front to back.

She grunted and looked frustrated as she shook her head in an attempt to say something.

"Don't worry, I understand; you relax and let me show you some more."

Was I doing the right thing? Was I adding to her frustration? *Act normal, Donna, so she stays calm. How do other people handle situations like this with loved ones?*

Her eyes looked at the bag of clothing and I took that as a sign she wanted to see more. "Fashion show is in full swing! Here is a black outfit with red trim. Pretty stylish top." I laid the outfit on the bed and pulled out a brown and tan set. "You look fabulous in brown. This outfit will... will be great." I almost slipped and said this outfit will look great on you when you go out to dinner. "The last outfit is the best! Your favorite color, Irish green." Holding it up, I turned it around so she could see the details.

First her eyes moistened and she made noises like whimpers that grew into sobbing while the upper part of her body trembled.

"Mom. Mom. Please. I love you. It's okay. I didn't mean to upset you. Relax. You're fine. I'm here." Holding her right hand, I watched for about ten minutes before she settled down. I gazed at her face, ravaged by years of alcohol abuse and smoking. To me she was beautiful, she was my mom. She sacrificed so much of her life for my brother and me. Maybe after she felt her children were going to be okay, the drinking buried her disappointments.

She started and stopped a few times but I think she was attempting to say, "Pretty," as she glanced at the green outfit. The speech therapist was convinced she could help her communicate with at least one word responses or short phrases. Sadly, her physical skills had not responded to treatment and essentially she was bedridden; however, with the use of a mechanical hoist, she could be lifted into a wheelchair to escape the confines of her room.

Was this her karma? Had her anger and the feeling of betrayal festered in her all these years? Had her divorce lowered her self-esteem because it wasn't accepted in the 50s? Did the disappointment of her horribly failed first marriage turn her to alcohol after her children were grown? Did the drinking distract her from internal growth, spiritual awareness, and fulfillment? I was desperately trying to understand my mother's feelings and passions. How could we heal if we didn't understand each other? Why hadn't I shared more of my experiences with her after I moved away? Why hadn't she expressed her fears and joy to me? I knew she hated her first husband, and I knew she loved John, whom she had married when I was seventeen, just before I left for college. What did my mother want for her life?

A thought becomes reality

John and I chatted in the morning over breakfast and then again when he arrived in the early evening at the nursing home. I was leaning against the wall in the hallway, trying to comprehend the repercussions of removing the feeding tube from my mother's stomach. My stepdad arrived every night after work, when his replacement arrived to manage the private club and bar he was president of, and stayed by Catherine's side until she had taken her medicine and fallen asleep. He never failed. I insisted he should take off a few evenings to rest because she couldn't possibility remember every single visit since her stroke. His answer was always the same, that he would know and he needed to be there for her. Would I ever find this kind of love and devotion? I hadn't even had a boyfriend that lasted longer than four years, let alone a guy who would be by my side if I were ill.

John wore his fedora hat and overcoat with style as he walked down the corridor, nodding and smiling at the staff and patients sitting in wheelchairs.

"Hi, Daddy, could I talk to you out here for a few minutes before you go in?"

"Sure, what is it? Is Catherine okay?" he asked with concern as he attempted to glance in her room to make sure his wife was still there.

Gingerly, I started, "She's fine. I spoke with her doctor to discuss our concerns about the recurring infection caused by the feeding tube. It's getting worse. Our options are limited: either continuing with the tube and battling the infection or removing it and hoping she can survive on mashed food, which could cause her to choke."

"Your mother doesn't have the immune system to combat an infection," he said, fidgeting with his overcoat. "There is no certainty she can swallow food either."

"This is not an easy decision, and I want to talk to Doug."

"Good, whatever he thinks, and you say, I will agree to," he said as he turned and entered Catherine's room. Watching him, I could see that John was beyond exhaustion. The role of caretaker had taken its toll, and I understood that he was afraid of making the wrong decision and somehow shortening his wife's life.

The next few days, I spent every waking minute with my mother while obsessing about the choice that had to be made.

Our ray of sunshine in an otherwise dismal situation came by way of the nursing home library. The room's warm wood paneling and cozy fireplace created a sanctuary for the home's residents. I pushed Mom's squeaky wheelchair into the library and could sense her excitement at seeing the shelves filled floor-to-ceiling with books. Once an avid reader, she loved everything about books. I invented a game of "Titles." I would read a title and she would nod her head yes or no, which indicated if she liked or disliked the name. Then I would ask if she had read the book. Yes or no? Did you like it? Yes or no? An easy game, it was a simple method of communicating. We played this game for hours—it kept her brain engaged until physically she needed to rest.

As her eyes browsed the racks of books, my thoughts drifted to George. *I wish you were alive. I need some help! You said I would heal with my mother, but you never said it would be like this. George, how do I know I will make the right decision? If the feeding tube is removed, will she die? Give me an answer! You said I could communicate with you on the other side, so show up and tell me what to do. I need a sign. NOW! Not next week. NOW!* I waited and watched and waited. Nothing, nada, zip.

After returning from the library, Mom was put back in bed by the staff and fell asleep. Walking outside, I sat down on a bench, away from the entrance, so I could be alone, punched my brother's number, and listened through several rings. The wind whipped at my face as I brought my coat up beneath my chin.

"Doug, Mom is okay, but let's consider the decision we discussed a few days ago. I need your input." Trembling, I said, "If the doctor removes the feeding tube, there's a chance she could choke, or she won't take in enough nutrition by mouth and could die."

"What do you think?" he said as his voice constricted.

I cleared my throat and continued, "She already has trouble breathing and swallowing. I discussed it with John. He wants us to make the decision. Did you know he's here every night? The other day when he was here, Mom said, 'ugly…no…makeup.' You know how hard it is for her to say only a few words." I became silent as I thought.

Doug said softly, "Go ahead, I am listening."

"His reply to her was, 'Catherine, you are beautiful the way you are. Those other ladies have to wear makeup to look half as pretty as you.'" Tears welled up in my eyes.

Doug said nothing.

"It's amazing how even in her feeble state, they reach out to each other," I said. "If anything happens to Mom, it would kill him."

"You can't think like that. If they take the tube out, what are her chances of dying?"

"I don't know. No one knows for sure if she..."

"Once again, do you think she could die?" he stated in his businessman tone.

"I don't know. Yes, I guess. She runs a fever every day. The infection could kill her."

"You'll have to make the decision for us both and help John." His voice softened as he continued. "Donna, I know you will make the right choice. You are there. You know her condition. I trust you."

Rather than getting angry with my brother for dumping this in my lap, I understood that I had talked to the doctors and nursing staff more about her condition, therefore I had the most recent information to make the intelligent decision. Being my big brother, he often disapproved of my choices. He was not at all supportive when I launched my speaking career, purchased my home, or adopted my daughter. He wanted me to follow a more conservative and traditional path. Hell, he had been married and divorced three times and was now heading for another marriage. Many times over the years I had felt his harsh judgment, and it hurt me deeply. Now he had to rely on me to make the right choice for all of us. Could it be that Doug and I were beginning to heal as well?

After hanging up, I opened my purse to put away my cell phone and noticed the mail that I had stuffed in there right before I left Tahoe. I had been so preoccupied that I had forgotten about it. I pulled out a letter from Rosella, my girlfriend from England, whom I considered an enlightened soul. Our paths had crossed years ago when I was speaking on a cruise ship where she was the activities director, and we remained friends ever since. I tore open the envelope and read, "Donna, I wrote these words to help you in your time of need."

The healing light does shine over you.
It is a warm bright light and it is made up of love,
the love that others bear for you when they pray
or when they wish you well.
Open to that healing light, feel it, and see it.
Let it sustain you when you are feeling low, giving you the hope,
the courage, the strength, and, of course, the healing. —Rosella

How kind of you, my friend, to reach out and lift my spirits, I thought. *Healing is what it's all about. Thank you for your words of encouragement.* The wind whisked past my ears as if whispering to me.

Lesson Learned:

Healing begins with little steps

Chapter Six

A Prediction from Above

Back in the home of my youth, memories flooded my mind as I climbed the steps to the third level. Loneliness is what I felt. This house was not the same without my mother. Oh, how I missed my daughter, too. I yearned to reach out and hold her.

After a restless night, I gave up on any real sleep and climbed out of bed at dawn. I showered, dressed, and packed my suitcase. Before closing my purse, I checked my plane ticket to confirm my four o'clock departure. Today would be my final visit to the nursing home before returning to Tahoe, and I dreaded making the decision that I couldn't put off any longer.

Mom looked beautiful in her new green outfit and was truly enjoying the compliments she was receiving from the staff. I watched as her lips parted slightly and a smile formed at the corners of her mouth. I had painted her nails a striking deep mauve and had her hair done at the salon in the nursing home. Would she live to wear more of her new clothes? Would my decision today shorten her life?

As I pushed her noisy wheel chair up and down the aisles of books in the library, playing our special game, my eyes kept wandering to the library clock. It was already late morning, and a decision had to be made. And soon. After returning to her room, the staff used the hoist to lift Mom back into her bed, and she drifted off to sleep quickly.

I stood frozen at the foot of her bed, occasionally glancing out the large-paned window at the bird feeder. *Decision. Decision. I need to make the correct decision.* Walking toward the window, I sensed I was being summoned by the massive church across the parking lot. The cathedral and I had a long history. I had attended services there with my biological father and Doug throughout my childhood. Sometimes I actually enjoyed it. Sunday school was fun, but the church sermons were too long. It was as if my father went there to repent, and I sensed his new-found self-esteem walking out of the building. The enormous church, an architectural prototype of the future, was simplistically designed, but life wasn't that simple.

I grabbed my jacket from the chair, slipped it on, and quietly left the room. My destination was the church. Could I find the answer I was looking for there?

I entered the First Presbyterian Church and was the only person inside as I slid into one of the benches closest to the altar. With high-beamed ceilings and an unadorned cross, the only traditional touch was in the form of jewel-toned light radiating through the stained glass windows. Folding my hands, I bowed my head and closed my eyes, reflecting on Mom's condition. What was she thinking about when her eyes were glazed over? Did she feel her life had been worthwhile? Had she accomplished what she wanted to? Had she completed her mission? Were her dreams realized?

Hmm… Maybe her dreams had shattered like waves on a craggy shore. But she fought, she struggled, she raised her kids with as many opportunities as she could possibly afford. Did she make that her mission?

Moreover, was that why she was so angry, upset, and unsupportive when I adopted my daughter as a single mom? Did she think that because she never would have chosen to raise us on her own that I should have understood the sacrifices and difficulties? Was she incredibly disappointed that I didn't "get it" and was determined to have my own way?

Stubborn—that was Mom. She wouldn't even talk to me on the phone. Of course, after she spent time with her granddaughter at John's 70th birthday party, Mariah had her wrapped around her little finger. A vivid image came to me of them sitting at the dining room table with oversized paint brushes. What a mess they made, but I loved the laughter. Mom had had only two years and a few visits to enjoy Mariah until she had her stroke. Paralyzed in a nursing home, undergoing alcohol and nicotine withdrawal, she was reviewing her life and coming to terms with her own shortcomings. George had insisted that everyone had to come to terms with their fears rather than being controlled by them. I believed that my mother was being forced to take a realistic look at what she had done. Would I have to do the same thing one day? Did every living person have to endure a reviewing process?

Noticing the pulpit and remembering the times I had fidgeted through services while sitting beside my father, Donald, during the turbulent years of my parents' divorce, I recalled the pain and the lies Doug and I experienced as the victims of my parents' hatred for one another. We always had to be with our father on weekends. Neither Doug nor I could ever make any other plans or be with our friends. When our cousins came from out of state to visit at our mother's, we had to leave with Father. He didn't care if it was family because it was not his side of the family tree. Even if I ran a temperature and threw up, my mother insisted I go with my father because she wouldn't allow him in her house to check on me. He never came to the front door, only blew his horn from the curb.

Pushing away my thoughts, I ran my fingers through my wavy short hair and silently began to pray. *Dear God, please help me make the proper decision for Mom. Please, guide me. I feel...I believe...I think her feeding tube should be removed.*

When you pray, you talk to God
When you meditate, God talks to you

I shivered, pushed my hands into my coat pockets, wriggled circulation back into my toes, and kept my vigil on the pew. Suddenly, adrenaline surged through my body. Then it happened, but not as I hoped. A message burst through my subconscious and left me stunned. *Your father will die in eight months.*

I took a shallow breath and blew it out. I must have misunderstood. I was emotionally upset, but I thought I was clear. I was asking about my mother, not my father. The message must be about her. Whatever I felt, it had to be about my mother. Eight months was more than we could hope for with the feeding tube, so removing it must be the right decision. That would give her until July. At least we would have more time to heal and John would have time to accept the loss of his partner. The message had come with such certainty, I was confident that removing the tube was the best course of action. I would make the arrangements with her doctor and the procedure could be carried out tomorrow.

I was sure, or was I? The message had to be about my mother, not my father. My father was in good health. I had seen him only a couple of weeks ago in Tahoe and he was fit as a fiddle. Ten years ago, he had moved to the lake area only fifteen minutes from my house. Our visits were short but cordial, but I still considered my real daddy to be John.

I left a voicemail on Doug's machine telling him the decision, and then I talked to John at work. I sensed he had his fears, but he didn't express them to me. He said to go ahead and tell the doctor. The only thing left to do was say my farewells to Mom.

Overwrought with emotions that I might not ever see her alive again, I kept stroking her hand. Fighting back tears, I whispered, "I love you. I am grateful you are my mom. I love you so much. I have always loved you." Why hadn't I said this to her more before she had the stroke? I should have tried harder to heal with my mother.

She stared at me, tilting her head slightly to the right. Slowly forcing her mouth to move and forming words, she said, "Love...you."

Leaving the nursing home, hot, wet tears streamed down my face as sobs escaped me.

An hour later I was at the Allentown-Bethlehem-Easton Airport longing to go back west and see Mariah. No wonder disappointment brought me to tears when the airline announced my flight was cancelled due to mechanical problems. I was on the verge of hysteria. The airline employee, comprehending my condition, was accommodating by offering a bus ride to Newark, New Jersey to catch another flight.

After the almost two-hour ride and upon my arrival in Newark, I was told turbulent rain storms were causing flight delays of three hours. When the boarding call finally echoed in my ears, my anxiety and agitation was in full swing. When I called home, Sara, the nanny, informed me there was almost a foot of snow on the ground and she didn't feel safe driving to Reno to pick me up.

"Sara, don't worry. I'll take a cab home," I voiced.

"That would be great and safer for Mariah too."

After landing in Reno and dragging my luggage through the deserted airport, I was shocked to see it was almost 5 AM. Standing before the taxi stand alone, I roused a sleepy driver; I inquired how much it would cost to my address in Tahoe.

He drowsily answered, "Sixty-five dollars."

"I only have fifty." The driver, a lanky fellow with a bald spot on the back of his head, gave me a disinterested glare. Though I tried to sound firm, my voice trembled as I said, "You can drop me off close to home and I'll catch a ride from there. Please, I need to get to my house. I have to hold my daughter."

He nodded. "Get in."

Settling into the back seat, like a rag doll, it took only a few minutes from the motion of the taxi and the grind of the engine to work like a sedative on my weary body.

I awoke with a jolt when I heard the driver say, "We're coming up on River Ranch."

When I saw the meter had ticked over sixty dollars, panic clawed at my chest and I yelled, "Stop! Stop right here! Don't go any farther. I only have fifty dollars. I'll walk from here!"

The driver swiveled his head around and said, "Lady, settle down. It's snowing."

I babbled hysterically, "I can't. I don't have any more money. I've got to get home to my daughter. Let me out." I kicked at the door and tried to push down on the handle.

The driver raised a hand and said, "Look, listen to me."

With a final push, the door opened and the wind whipped it out of my hands as the taxi still moved.

"Lady, close the door. Will you watch what I'm doing!" He flipped down the flag on the meter. "I won't charge you more than fifty dollars. Now, tell me how far you live from here?"

"Oh, oh, very kind." After several frustrating yanks on the car door, I managed to get it closed. *Oh, God, I'm out of control.* "About...about four miles," I sobbed.

"Pay me what you have." He gave me an odd look through the rearview mirror, like he knew my hold on reality was slipping. "When was the last time you slept?"

"In the back seat," I mumbled. "I flew in from Pennsylvania. I...I was in the nursing home with my... I'd guess I've been awake for over twenty-four hours."

He nodded. "Don't worry. I'll get you home to your daughter safe and sound."

"Thank you," I said softly.

The clock on the dashboard signaled the time as I clasped my fingers tightly together, not from cold, but to pray. It was 6 AM, so it would be 9 AM back east, and the doctor would be prepping to remove the feeding tube.

Lesson Learned:

Ask for guidance

Part II

Healing on Overtime

Chapter Seven
The Blue Dress

The first trip to Disneyland is as captivating to a child as Dorothy visiting the Land of Oz. It was the end of June and it was time for fun. I had coordinated my work schedule to coincide with the trip so Mariah and I could celebrate her fifth birthday together at the enchanted world of Disney, and she was as pumped up as a kid could be.

I had visited my mom several times since the feeding tube was removed, and her condition remained stable. She was still at the nursing home, receiving twenty-four-hour care. The staff fed her mashed-up food, which Mother ate, but she didn't like the green-colored mush since she was sure it tasted like vegetables and she despised vegetables. On my visits I spent hours in the dining hall feeding her lunch and dinner. It took patience. Because of her condition, she had to drink and eat very slowly, and I marveled at how kind and persistent the staff was to ensure Catherine received enough nourishment. During my last trip, my doubts and uncertainty about us healing had dissipated after my mom uttered, "You...great mom. Good...Mariah..." Those simple words made all the difference. My next visit back east would be in July, and I was looking forward to it.

Inside the park, my daughter twirled around in her own little animated world, exclaiming, "Mommy, there's Mickey and Minnie! Look! Over there. It's Goofy! Please take my picture with Goofy!" She dragged me by the hand toward a crowd of children lined up to pose with the big floppy-eared dog. After sweltering in the hot sun for twenty minutes, Mariah's wish for a photo with her pal Goofy was granted. Her eyes sparkled with joy as she hugged Goofy and then bounced away with her feet almost floating along the pavement.

As the afternoon wore on, the temperature climbed and the lines elongated. I felt tired and blamed it on the trips back to Pennsylvania and my work schedule. Lack of sleep was normal for me. Rolling my neck, I pushed the queasy feeling I had in my stomach out of my mind. I forced a smile and squeezed Mariah's hand, signaling to her that we were moving up in the long line for Mr. Toad's Wild Ride, and our turn would be soon. I kept getting hotter and started fanning myself with my hand. Minutes later, I keeled over.

Two park employees quickly guided me away from the inquisitive stares of other park patrons to a shady area, and Mariah kneeled close by with a questioning expression on her face, holding onto my arm. I was a mom and didn't want to worry my daughter—she was concerned enough about her Nana—so on with the show. I braved a smile that wasn't quite there, and though my skinned hands screamed in pain from the fall I had just taken, I pulled her to me in a big hug and said, "Look, Mariah! I'm not hurt! All better now. I just need to rest a bit."

After sitting still a few more minutes and gathering some deep breaths, I struggled to my feet, and though my heart wasn't in it, I resumed the adventure. An employee moved us to the front of the Mr. Toad line and Mariah squealed with delight. We managed to enjoy several more rides: The Mad Tea Party, It's a Small World, and the Carousel, which turned out to be Mariah's favorite. I had to admit that her laughter and nonstop chatter were infectious. Her face illuminated by a huge smile while she sat on a toothy white carousel horse, yelling,

"Faster! Giddy up! Go faster!" as I clutched her squirming little body. My heart overflowed with joy as I watched her bob up and down while we went around in circles. Resting after every ride helped before heading on to the next escapade.

Life is precious
Have fun like a child

The tram ride through the park was next. After passing Fantasyland, Frontierland, and New Orleans Square, Mariah could hardly sit still when we disembarked at the Pirates of the Caribbean boat ride.

"Pirates! Pirates!" Mariah exclaimed as we entered the haunted caves. She covered her eyes while screaming at the scary parts, all the while clutching my arm. When she got off the ride, she turned in circles, shouting how much she loved Disneyland.

It was getting to be early evening. *How am I ever going to get this child out of the amusement park?* Heaving a sigh of relief when I came across an empty bench, I sat down to fan myself with a park map while Mariah hopped from one foot to the other. This was an important day for both of us, supposed to be filled with nothing but carefree entertainment. I had booked a long trip for Mariah and me to visit Bethlehem in July, but right now I needed to enjoy this day and laugh with my child. The trips back east had taken their toll. Leaving Mariah at home with the nanny or dragging her along and then dropping her at a babysitter's house all day left me guilt-stricken from the time I walked out the door until I returned. Lurking in the back of my mind was the premonition that my mother would die in eight months—it was June now, and July, the eighth month, was around the corner. Yet I couldn't shake the memory that it was my father's name I had heard.

"Mommy, let's get an ice cream cone. I want chocolate!"

A nice cold ice cream cone sounded like a good idea. Walking across the bridge leading past Sleeping Beauty's Castle, Mariah's eyes lit up.

"Look, a real castle! Let's go inside."

"Honey, it's only for shopping."

"Please. Pretty please. Let's go inside!"

Mariah pulled my hand, tugging me into the gift shop. The place was dress-up paradise for a child, and Mariah was the dress-up belle of our household. Colored costumes of sapphire, crimson, amber, and emerald adorned the racks lining the walls. A cartload of accessories were on display for Cinderella, Little Mermaid, and Sleeping Beauty ensembles: tiaras, slippers, gloves, wands, and a vast array of little luxuries documented on screen by our cherished Disney films. Typical of a five-year-old, Mariah made a beeline for the glitz. The sparkle in her eyes took on new meaning as she stood mesmerized at Cinderella's beautiful blue and pearly white satin dress and matching white gloves. Her head tilted to one side and then the other as her small fingers reached out to delicately stroke the fabric of the dress.

Nothing would have made me happier than to buy the gown, but when I saw the price tag of the fetching ensemble, I said, "C'mon, Mariah, let's get that ice cream cone."

She didn't move or take her eyes off the costume. With conviction in her voice she stated, "I must have this blue dress."

I certainly could understand her wanting the evening gown. It was gorgeous, every little girl's dream, but I did not have an extra hundred dollars to spend on a fantasy wardrobe. I replied, "Coming to Disneyland was your birthday present. We're going to get our ice cream, but the dress is not in my budget today."

With a determined look, Mariah said, "But Mommy, I must have the blue dress."

"Mariah," I said firmly, "the dress is beautiful, and I really do understand how much you wish it was yours, but I can't afford to buy it." I took her by the hand and we left the shop. Outside, she stopped dead in her tracks.

Sounding even more resolute, she said, "Mommy, I must have the blue dress."

"Do you want ice cream or a snack?" I asked, beginning to tire of the drama. I knew my daughter could be dramatic, but this was even over the top for her.

"I don't want ice cream! I don't want a snack!" she stated and crossed her arms.

"Would you like to go on another ride?"

"No. I want the dress."

Even at five years old, she knew that as long as she kept spinning the wheel, there was always the chance she'd come out a winner. Taking a moment to think, I tried to figure out a tactic that would work in my favor, because I felt myself caving in.

"I don't want ice cream. I'll wear the dress for Halloween. I must have the blue dress!"

"Hold up," I stated, as gently as I could, deciding to apply a more analytical strategy. "Why is the dress so important to you?"

"I must have the blue dress."

Why was she being so adamant? I figured that my next approach would get her to acquiesce. "Let me explain something. If we buy the dress, we're done here. Are you sure you're okay with that? Bye-bye Mickey, Minnie, and Goofy. No food either; we're out of here, right away."

Sure, she would plead and beg at times, but give up Disneyland, no way. Her unblinking hazel eyes gazed directly into mine, and with a certainty that belied a young child, she said, "It's okay to leave right after we buy the dress."

She took my stunned silence as a "yes," running back into the shop before I could open my mouth to stop her. By the time I caught up with her, Mariah was standing in front of the dress, waiting. *Okay,* I thought, *if I'm purchasing this costume, she is going to get some wear out of it.* I chose a larger size, figuring with some alterations Mariah could wear it for years. I ended up buying the entire ensemble, right down to the fake glass slippers.

Grinning from ear to ear, Mariah stood on tiptoes, overseeing the items being packaged into a large logo bag. "I'll carry it," she announced.

As we exited the park, I found it hard to believe that there wasn't a single complaint from my daughter. She didn't even glance over her shoulder.

In the back seat of the car, she reached into the bag every so often to touch her precious new dress and reassure herself that all the Cinderella stuff was still inside. I was mystified and kept thinking of one of my mentor's Georgeisms.

Everything happens for a reason
There are no accidents

Accelerating onto the freeway, I winced as my skinned hands gripped the steering wheel, and I thought back to my spill in the park. What an interesting day—first, I fainted and then what was it that had led us to the irresistible blue dress? Was there something yet to be revealed?

Lesson Learned:
Have the faith of a child

Chapter Eight
Prince Charming Arrives

A couple of weeks after visiting Disneyland, I held an impromptu family gathering in my abundantly blossoming backyard to celebrate mine and my father's birthdays and my brother's marriage to his wife, Donna. Doug and his wife drove from San Francisco and were staying at his mountain home in Squaw Valley for a long weekend.

Of all the names on the planet, Doug had to marry a woman with the same name as mine. I liked her; why not—we shared a name. Donna the elementary school teacher was organized, outgoing, and petite.

There were so many marriages and divorces in our family; it might explain why I never made the commitment. Father was married three times, my mother twice, and with his latest marriage to Donna, my brother four times, so I guess marriage was not on my horizon if I was to lower the family average. I had designed my wedding dress a few times. I had an incredible imagination, and that is where my wedding would stay—in my fantasy world. I had dated dozens of guys and had marriage proposals, but the fear of being controlled by a man kept me from taking the plunge.

Weather-wise, the day of the party couldn't have been more ideal.

Sunshine streamed through the pines, reflecting off the surface of the indigo lake. The vivid colors of summer—white, yellow, purple and a brilliant orange—were plentiful throughout the backyard.

Suddenly, Mariah jumped up from her play kitchen. "Poppy's fancy car is here," she shouted as she threw open the front door, racing towards her grandfather.

She unleashed a childish giggle, then said, "Poppy! Poppy. My Poppy!"

He bent down, hugging her. "How's my girl doing?"

My father, who lived in Nevada with an exquisite view of Lake Tahoe and only a twelve-mile drive from my home, was a man of reserved emotions. Being in his eighties and raised the only child in a conservative eastern family, he greeted me with a warm hello and a peck on the cheek. I thought, *He looks good, healthy, enjoying his life, like he should at his age.* He was of a stocky build, but not heavy, and his mostly-gray hair had some brown, which he combed to cover the thinning parts.

Father's wife, Barbara, walked in right behind him. She was attractive, had a short hair style with not a strand out of place, and dressed in the latest fashion, including matching shoes. Our relationship was respectful yet cool.

We passed the afternoon in the backyard chatting over iced tea and munchies. I gazed at my father sitting across from me and asked, "So, how was your trip?"

"It was fantastic, actually, great. My wife and I had an incredible time. Mexico is different, but I love it there. Very soothing in the condo we bought. I like looking at the ocean." He smiled at Barbara. "Of course, I think I like it more than my wife. Language barrier, but I am not afraid to use my hands to get my point across or ask a question."

He carried on with plenty of enthusiasm about their time in Mexico, what they saw, where they went. Father was the center of attention, which he always liked to be as he held court from his lawn chair. He never asked about what Mariah was up to, or how I was doing, but that was Father. Why should I expect anything else? Memories bubbled to the surface, but I quickly squelched them. I didn't want to think about our past; I only wanted to relish this afternoon. Doug, Donna, Barbara, Mariah, and I listened and didn't say a word. Finally, He turned to Barbara and smiled again. Then, clearing his throat, he continued, "I guess this is as good a time as any to talk about my cataract surgery. I haven't been seeing too well lately and I've done something about it. I've scheduled to have my eyes done the day after my birthday, July 13th."

"That's pretty normal, isn't it? Your mother had it done and she lived to be 101," Doug, who was very much like Father, stated.

As they interacted, I observed how physically similar they were—both were around 5'8" with a stocky physique, round faces, and fair skin. Not only were they physically alike, but their work values were the same, since my brother spent so much time helping our father in his background music business. He understood the clients, the products, the time frame, and the cost to install the background piped-in music in offices and stores and the cycle of billing. They brainstormed ideas, and Father and Doug even bought separate franchises to a digital communication sign company.

I knew I was way closer to my stepdad than my father. I enjoyed spending time with John; he had a calming effect on me. Being with my father caused me to tense, to feel depressed. Was it because he was never the kind, warm, and caring father I wished for, or was there too much unresolved history between us?

I brought my focus back to the present. Father said, "So I'm told. My only concern is that I'll have to go off my blood thinner medication a couple days before surgery. The eye doctor assures me it's a common outpatient procedure and I'll be home the same day. I'm feeling uneasy. I need to correct my vision, but I still don't like surgery," he insisted with concern in his voice.

"You're in good health. Aren't you planning another trip soon?" I questioned.

"Yes, that's why I'm having the operation. We're going to New Zealand and Australia this fall."

"I believe this is a good time for your father to have his surgery before we go on any other trips," his wife stated as she bobbed her head.

My father commenced another lengthy monologue about their upcoming vacation, and I excused myself to refresh our snacks. Mariah followed me and made a beeline for her bedroom.

"Mommy, you gotta come in here!" Her voice grew louder as she added a whine. "Mommy, pleeease," she called out as I replenished the cheese and cracker tray.

"Not now, I'm busy," I answered. "Come to the backyard again!" When there was only silence, I headed toward her room to see what the little darling was up to. As I entered, I saw her squirming into the Cinderella gown.

"Please, help me with the choker and gloves."

Recalling the Disneyland theatrics, I decided a relaxed approach would be best. "Honey, must you do this now? Wouldn't it be better to wait until later?"

"You don't understand. I want to show this dress to Poppy and everyone. I must. I just must." She thrust the gloves at me like royalty bestowing a ladyship.

Squeezing her little hands into the long gloves was not an easy task. I hooked on the choker and stood back to gaze at the dazzling transformation. "You look beautiful. Just like Cinderella."

She whispered, "Guess who my Prince Charming is?"

"I don't know. Tell me," I said, joining in the game.

She beamed, hoisting her dress up off the floor, and prepared to leave the room. Fake glass slippers clomping on the carpet, she giggled, "Poppy is my Prince Charming."

I experienced a flush of motherly pride and found myself wishing my mom could be here to witness this, instead of in a nursing home. I knew it would brighten her day to see Mariah model her beautiful dress-up gown. When I was Mariah's age, my mother's mother, Nana, handmade a brilliant yellow Spanish costume with black lace and an extravagant headpiece for the Halloween Parade. The next year I was decked out in green like an Irish lass with a flouncy bonnet. Make-believe ran in the family.

Returning to the patio, Mariah wasted no time in pulling her grandfather by the hand toward a wooden bench. "Poppy, help me up," she begged as she held her dress bunched in her little hands, with her glass slippers in full view.

He lifted her onto the bench and stepped back. Mariah smoothed out her gown until she was satisfied she looked like a true princess. What happened after that was so astonishing that it made tears well up in my eyes.

Father played his princely character by getting down on one knee and holding Mariah's hand. The father I remembered was all business, and children with foolish make-believe games were not tolerated. Competitive sports were the focus; so I played tennis, snow skied, rode horses, and even did archery, but no silly play was allowed. My brother was athletic, so he did all the same sports I did but a little better than me. Poppy with his granddaughter endeared a softness I had never seen before. Picking up my camera, I began clicking away, shooting picture after picture of Cinderella and Prince Charming.

The afternoon turned out to be one of the better times I had with my family. Before father left, he pulled me aside and handed me an envelope. He softly said, "This is for Mariah's education fund. Let's keep it between us. Don't say anything to Barbara. I don't want to upset her."

"Father…" I protested.

"It's not much, only $100, but add it to her college fund. If anything happens to me, make sure Mariah gets a good education."

"Don't talk like that. You're healthy as an ox."

"I know. I know. But it's only natural to be a little worried. You and Doug are provided for in my will. You'll have money for Mariah's education."

"Please, stop worrying. You'll be fine." I hugged him. "Thank you. It's kind of you to contribute to my daughter's future."

He nodded and hugged me back. "Donna, I had a good time."

Make every day count
Live in the present

Watching them pull out of the driveway, I wondered if George had been correct in telling me that someday I would heal with my mother, father, and brother. I was healing with my mother. She had accepted that I was a good mom. Now, could it be time to heal with my father? I had never seen him so kind before. For over twenty years I had prayed for healing with my family, and now I was starting to believe it would happen. How was it supposed to play out?

Lesson Learned:

Let magic happen

Chapter Nine

This Can't Be Happening

When the weather is flawless and the sky a cloudless palette of blue, there is no better place than the tranquility of summer in Tahoe. I cherished living here in July. No snow—well, usually no snow. The morning hours flew by as I spent the time tailoring a speech for a healthcare client. My business was puttering along at this point—the many visits back east to be with my mother had taken their toll, and my marketing had slipped, as had my income. Money would come later, I hoped. Right now, my commitment was to heal with my mom.

After a macaroni-and-cheese lunch with my daughter, I stood at the kitchen sink, washing off dishes. The backyard was exquisite with the blue spruce tree and white daisies dancing in the gentle summer breeze. Hanging up the dish towel, my eye caught Mariah's crayon drawing of her and the cat taped to the refrigerator door. I softly giggled, recalling her words. "Sisters don't need to look alike. They only have to love each other. Sheba is my sister." How different they seemed, but maybe not. Sheba, a fluffy white Himalayan with stunning gray markings, was very mellow, whereas Mariah was a powerhouse of energy with sparking eyes, short brown hair, fair skin and tall for her age. Yet both had kind souls, loved to curl up on the sofa, and were extremely patient with each other.

A sudden chill ran up my spine. *What was that?* I instinctively sent out a question, having learned to trust my intuition. When George had visited Tahoe, he had given me the gift of intuition in the form of mysterious envelopes and insisted I develop and honor that ability. I turned around and saw Mariah at the table coloring. Surrounded by crayons and pastel construction paper, she was chattering away describing what she was drawing. *Alright, my daughter is safe.* Next I looked for the cat. Sheba was curled up on the sofa right behind Mariah. *She's fine.* Had something happened to mother? *No.* To my stepdad? *No.* Father? Nothing came to me. I asked again. Father? The seconds ticked away in silence.

I spun around and stared at the clock; it was 1:33 PM. This was the day of his eye operation. He should be home by now, since he was scheduled for an early morning outpatient surgery. A weird sensation tingled throughout my body.

The phone at his home rang endlessly before the voicemail answered. Sounding upbeat and confident, I left a message to call right away and let me know how he was doing. Maybe they stopped for a bite to eat. I waited for twenty-five minutes, punched the redial button on the phone, but still no answer. After three more calls, my uneasy feeling began to amplify. I couldn't shake it. Dialing my brother's number, the sensation in my stomach heightened. My brother spent more time with Father than me—they worked together on special projects and went out to dinners, so maybe he knew where Father was right now. He might have even spoken to him today.

"They're a little late. What are you worried about?" Doug said, sounding annoyed. "They probably stopped to do some shopping in Reno or they went to his office to pick up something."

"For God's sake, Doug, he had surgery. Father is 81 and he'd be too woozy from the anesthesia to do anything except go right home. What do you think I should do?"

"I think you should stop worrying. As I said, he might have needed something at the office."

"I know how wrapped up he is in the business, but even he has his limitations," I protested.

Doug sighed at the other end of the line. "What do you want from me? Do you want me to call the office?"

"Yes."

"I'll get back to you."

"Soon. Thanks."

Attempting to go back to work, I couldn't concentrate, couldn't rid myself of the dreadful feeling that something was very wrong.

On the first ring, I grabbed the phone. "Did you find out anything?"

"Yes." A long, uncomfortable pause from the other end of the phone.

"What? Where are they?"

"Donna, I don't want to upset you, but I have some bad news. I called the office and tracked down Barbara. She's at the hospital with him."

Expelling a rush of air from my lungs, I asked, much more calmly than I felt, "He's at the hospital?"

"Yes. Let me give you the details, then ask questions."

My personality wouldn't allow me wait as I began asking, "Is he okay?"

"No."

"What's wrong?"

"The eye surgery went fine, but after they came home, he had a stroke. His wife called an ambulance and they rushed him to Saint Mary's Hospital in Reno. He's in Intensive Care."

"Intensive Care." I leaned against the wall for support. *This can't be happening. First Mother, now Father. Both downed by strokes.* "Is he going to live?"

"I don't know. He's listed as stable."

"I need to see him. I'm going to drive down there."

"Hold up. He's under the care of a team of doctors. Barbara was adamant that you should not visit the hospital because she doesn't want you upsetting him."

"Upsetting him! He's my father."

"She promised to keep us updated," Doug stated flatly.

It wasn't difficult to envision my father lying helpless in a hospital bed after the experience with my mother. Tears streamed down my cheeks. "I'm driving down the mountain to see him."

"If that's the way you feel, then go, but know that his wife does not want you there."

"It's not about her, it's about our father. I'll call you later," I said, irritated. I called Sara, the nanny, who came over as soon as she could. Scooping up Mariah, I smothered her with kisses. "Buttercup, Mommy has to run to Reno for a little while, but you can play with Sara."

"Okay, Mommy, see you soon. Will miss you," she said, engrossed in her artwork.

The nanny, a college grad who was young, slender, with long blonde hair, instantly sat with Mariah to distract her from my leaving. I mouthed to her, "father" and "hospital." Sara shook her head slightly. She understood I didn't want to say anything to my daughter.

As I sped up the ramp leading into the parking structure at the hospital, the rosy orb of the setting sun dipped behind the Sierras and the soft shadows of early evening were already present. Each step toward Intensive Care sent my panic a notch higher. Nearing the nurse's station, I muttered, "Donald Hartley is my father. Is he here?"

The nurse behind the desk nodded and said, "He is."

I spoke forcefully, "Is his doctor available?"

She glanced toward the end of the counter, where a tall balding man was standing. As if sensing my presence, he swiveled his head in my direction, his heavily lidded eyes peering at me inquiringly.

"Don Hartley is my father. Can you tell me his condition?"

He nodded, but before he could answer, the nurse interrupted, telling him that Mrs. Hartley was on the phone and insisted she talk to him now.

Reaching over, he picked up the phone. "Mrs. Hartley. Good timing, your daughter has arrived."

Several minutes passed before he glanced at me, brows knitted tightly together. It didn't take a MENSA genius to guess what she was saying to him.

"Well...uh-huh...I see. Yes...yes hang on, please." The doctor handed the phone to me. "She would like to speak to you."

I took the phone from him and said, "Hello."

"I asked your brother to tell you not to come to the hospital and that I would keep you informed. Your father needs his rest." Her voice was whiny, high-pitched, and loud.

"He's alone. Someone should be with him." I felt a strange lightness, like I was experiencing déjà vu. My mother downed with a stroke, now my father. I couldn't wait; I understood how precious time is.

"I was with him all day," Barbara stated.

I wasn't going to wait for permission that would not come. "That's my father lying in there and I intend to be with him, no matter what you say," I declared. She hung up. Turning around, I looked for the doctor, who had conveniently disappeared. I guess I couldn't blame him.

Without waiting for permission from the nurse or staff, I turned and walked into Father's room, where he lay motionless. His chest rose and fell as he labored for each breath. An oxygen mask covered his face, and he appeared to have shrunk since I last saw him. Even his hair seemed grayer and his skin paler than I remembered. Hadn't I endured this with my mother? Both parents...a stroke. They hadn't spoken since the divorce, when I was only six. Their animosity was relentless and here they are, only a year apart, with the same health issues. Had they both held too much anger in their hearts? Had their bodies been affected by their hatred?

I pulled the only chair close to the bed and sat down. Words swam around inside my head, but I was speechless. I gently took his hand in mine and softly said, "It's Donna. Can you hear me? I'm right here." There was no reaction, no movement, no eyelids fluttering, nothing. "I want to believe you can hear me," I said and struggled to think of what to say next.

What could I say to this man...my father? My mind transported me back to my teenage years, when I finally gained my father's admiration by winning ski races. I won lots of races. This acceptance was short-lived, however, when one Sunday I was late for snow ski practice.

Father had bought me a 49 Hudson for $100 and that was my transportation from my mother's house to his. That Sunday, I left Mother's home at 7 AM, only to have the car break down three times. When I walked into his home near the ski hill four hours late for practice, his backhand sent me flying across the room a dozen times, injuring my ribs to the point that the pain was almost unbearable. This was worse than the other times.

I ran to my bedroom, locked the door, and crouched in the closet, crying for over an hour. I hid there, unsure of what to do, until a thought flashed through my brain. Gary, a student in my senior English class, had told me before class last week that he was driving to Split Rock Ski Area this Sunday to ski. We had chatted about the snow and the area, because that's where I trained every weekend.

Sometime within the last hour I had spent in the closet, I heard Father slam his bedroom door, so sneaking out of my bedroom, I went to the phone in the kitchen and dialed the base lodge at the ski area, hoping—more like praying—Gary would be there. I had him paged, and then I waited. And waited. Really, what were the chances he would be in the ski mountain lodge at the exact time I paged him? Plus, Gary was quiet and shy, so he might not want to become involved and pick me up, even if my father's home was only a few miles from the ski area.

I felt a tension headache brewing. My ribs still felt bruised from where Father had hit me, and even breathing was difficult. I waited for probably only five minutes, but it seemed like eternity as I continually twisted the phone cord, scared to death my father would hear me and come out from his bedroom.

Relieved when I heard Gary's voice on the phone, I spoke softly as I told him I was in trouble and needed to get out of this house and home to my mom's. I almost blubbered when he ask for directions and said he was on his way.

During the days and months that followed, I accepted the reality that my ski career was over, since neither I nor Mom had the money to support this expensive sport. I promised myself my father would never physically or emotionally hurt me again—that was the last time. His behavior had always kept me in a state of perplexity. His up-and-down mood swings had me on edge, never knowing if he was going to be Mr. Hyde or Dr. Jekyll. I made a commitment to myself that no man would ever betray me or hurt me again.

About ten years ago, Father had received a business opportunity that brought him from the east coast to Lake Tahoe, Nevada. The fact that he accepted it made me feel that he had a hidden agenda. He was getting older, and I think that on some level he wanted to spend more time with me and heal the past—that is, of course, without talking about the past. I wasn't quick to forget or forgive; from my point of view, our relationship was guarded. But what shocked me was that Father seemed to cherish the idea of being a grandfather to Mariah, his only grandchild, although their time together was stifled by his jealous wife. I always felt Barbara wanted the attention and money to be spent on her instead of a grandchild, so my father stopped by for short solo visits to see Mariah and, who knows, maybe me, too.

Focusing on my father in the hospital bed, I straightened my spine and said, "Thank you…thank you for bringing me to Lake Tahoe for the Winter Olympics. I don't think I ever told you, but that trip changed my life. I know I was only in seventh grade, but when I was in the little stained-glass church in Squaw Valley, I asked that I would someday live in Tahoe. My request was answered. I feel blessed living here."

Was it possible to put the fears and disappointments of our strained relationship behind me? My mentor, whom I called so many names—Mr. Wise Man, Mr. Sage, and even Mr. Miracle Man—said we would heal, but like this? I know this was the eleventh hour but was it possible? I thought my father and I would have a conversation, something meaningful. My father and I never talked about anything of depth;

superficial topics were his strong suit. Lifting his hand and giving it a squeeze, I suddenly froze. Maybe I imagined it, but I swore I felt his fingers curl around mine.

Let go of the past
You only have now

All week long I spent the early hours of the morning, before sunrise and the very late night hours, sneaking into the hospital to visit my own father. Even after he had been moved to a private room, Barbara instructed the hospital staff I was not to visit. It took some coordination with my nanny, Sara, especially since she was preparing to move back home to New Zealand, but I did it.

Why was his third wife so threatened by me? Was her own radar telling her I had a strong intuition that indicated that all was not as it appeared to be? Sure, my brother was allowed to visit, and he did, but I was never officially permitted.

Standing by my father's hospital bed at 5 AM, seven days after his stroke, I sensed I should stay there all day instead of flying off to Bend, Oregon to present my speech, "Fire Up Your Life!" I didn't want to leave his bedside. I didn't feel like firing up anyone. What would my father do if the roles were reversed? I know what he would do: leave and go to work.

My mind flipped back to when I was sixteen, when Father dropped me off at a hospital an hour and a half from home to have surgery on my heart. After filling out the paperwork, he just left.

At a routine checkup at school to clear me for cheerleading, the doctor had heard a slight heart murmur. My mother took me to a specialist, who said to wait and observe and that nothing needed to be done at that time. My father wouldn't take the specialist's word, so off I went to another doctor to be examined. This doctor recommended heart surgery—a procedure called a heart catheterization, where a catheter would be inserted into a chamber of my heart for investigational purposes. First, they would puncture the femoral artery in the groin and a guide wire would be inserted and forced up to the heart chamber to check the blood flow in and out of the valves.

Father slapped a court order on my mother for neglect and banned me from cheerleading or doing any other sports. It was yet another battle between the parents, and again I was the pawn.

Agreeing that I would go with my father and have the operation, not wanting to. But I needed my life back—plus, I couldn't stand the fighting between my parents, since I had to deliver the messages that flew between them. Doug was at the University of Montana; it was all on me.

As I watched Father's retreating back through the doors of that hospital in Philadelphia, I realized I was alone in a strange town, with doctors I didn't know, about to go through a three-hour heart procedure and recovery all by myself. Seven days later, Father returned to pick me up at the hospital.

What if my daughter ever needed surgery? I couldn't even imagine leaving her for one second. In fact, I would sleep in the chair beside her bed for her entire stay in the hospital. *Maybe, just maybe, like George said, I am changing the patterns of my family. I had to be older and more mature before I became a mother. I'm not blaming my father, and I am not perfect by any means. My father did the best he knew how at the time, but it wasn't the best for me. It left scars. I choose to be different with my daughter.*

His wheezing through the oxygen mask drew me out of my thoughts. There was no change in his condition, still unconscious and wrestling for every breath. He appeared so frail. How could this man have caused so much pain in my life? If I were to be honest with myself, he was probably the reason I never married, fearing I would end up with a man like him. I had desperately wanted to marry, but on some level I understood I had too much baggage.

I stood near his bed for a long time, knowing that if I were ever to move forward in my life and have healthy relationships, I needed to forgive my father for all the beatings, lies, and betrayals. Choking back tears, I softly said, "I forgive you." Time passed in silence. "I love you." Sobbing, I slipped from the room.

The sensation I had the next day while speaking was that I wasn't all present. My brain was in a fog. Part of me was on the stage in Oregon, taking my audience on a journey of laughter and drama, while another part of me was in Reno by my father's bedside. Somehow my speech successfully concluded, and when back in my hotel packing my suitcase, a jarring sound sliced through my nerves. I lunged for the phone. I squeezed my eyes shut and prepared for the worst when I heard who was on the line.

"Donna. This is Barbara. I have come to a decision. It's what your father would want. I've asked the doctors to take Don off of oxygen and they've agreed."

I bristled at her statement. I said defensively, "I...I realize father would not want to live like a vegetable. It's been only eight days. It's too soon!"

Her reply was a jumble of words that made no sense to me. Her final statement was that this is what she had decided and it was done.

"Done?" I stood clutching the phone in my hand, listening only to the dial tone. She could have waited for his son and daughter. She could have asked our opinion first. There was no crisis requiring a life or death decision. Dialing my brother's number, I kept repeating to myself, *Answer, damn it, answer!*

"Did you hear about Father?" I shrieked into the phone.

"Yeah. Got the call a few minutes ago and gave her your number. I'm driving to Reno and it should take me about four hours. When does your flight get in?"

"At 4:00 PM. Will he be okay without oxygen?"

"I don't know. I'll see you there. I'm leaving right now," he said, sounding panicked.

My brother had always had a fairly decent relationship with Father, and had worked in his communication music business off and on since he was a teenager. Father didn't hit him like he did me—Doug wouldn't have tolerated it. Doug might not be very emotional, but I was sure that not being consulted about his father today upset him. I knew he felt the bonds of blood were stronger than the bonds of a third marriage—he had a say in the matter of his father's health.

At the airport, I saw that my flight had been delayed. *Delayed, no it can't be delayed. I need to be with my father.* I rushed to the check-in counter and begged for information. "Is there another flight? Another airport I can drive to? My father is in the hospital in critical condition. I have to be in Reno. Please, check for me!"

The helpful young clerk scanned her computer for a good five minutes and said, "I'm sorry, there's nothing else available. The flight you're booked on is the only one scheduled for this afternoon. The mechanics are working as fast as they can and the plane will depart as soon as it is ready."

Nodding, I turned away to find an empty seat because I knew the drill—sit and wait. I didn't last two minutes in the chair before I was up on my feet watching the clock. Time had never moved more slowly. When the boarding call finally came two hours later, I jumped, picked up my bag, took three steps, and halted in my tracks. Like water gushing in a flood channel, uncontrollable tears cascaded down my cheeks. *Father. Oh, no. Father.* I grabbed my cell phone, but it was dead. My voice thick with tears, I said to the attendant, "Don't close the gate until I get back. Please. I need to call the hospital. My father." I ran toward the bank of pay phones.

Saint Mary's Hospital switchboard transferred me to the nurses' station on Father's floor. I blurted out, "I'm Donna Hartley, Don Hartley's daughter. What is my father's condition?"

"I'm sorry, I can't give you that information. You need to speak to his wife."

"Okay, fine. Put her on."

"Uhhh...she's not here."

Where is she?

Clutching the receiver, I begged, "Look, I'm in Bend, Oregon, on my way to Reno. I need to know my father's condition before I board the plane. Please!"

There was a long pause before she said, "Your father passed away a few minutes ago. I'm sorry."

"Alone?" I asked, but I heard nothing. My voice barely audible, I squeaked, "Thank you." Leaning against the booth for support, through a haze of grief, I heard a woman's voice over the PA system, "Final call."

I trudged toward the gate, handed her my ticket, and headed out onto the tarmac in a light rain as my tears mixed with the raindrops. Boarding the small aircraft slowly, I gazed down at my ticket to find my seat number. The date on the ticket grabbed my attention. It was July 21st. *July. Oh my God, the intuitive flash I had back in November while sitting in the church in Pennsylvania told me my father would die in eight months; July. It was true, it wasn't my mother, but my father. I cast away that insight, rationalizing that it must be my mother, because she was the one who was sick and in the nursing home. My father was in good health. Why hadn't I listened? Why hadn't I trusted my intuition? Would I have done anything different?*

Lesson Learned:

Forgiveness is powerful

Chapter Ten

Going Backwards

The day had arrived to say a final goodbye to our father. Though I tried not to think about it, neither Doug nor I were asked to participate in the planning of the funeral. It left us both feeling like outsiders rather than his children; however, we were asked if we would like to say a few words at the service, which I agreed to do.

The funeral home was somber, with muted tones and plush carpet. I had to admit, he was getting a good send-off. Barbara had ordered the crème de la crème of caskets, and no expense had been spared on the lavish display of colorful floral arrangements. How was I supposed to feel? Should I say thank you to my father? I had enjoyed the opportunity to participate in all kinds of sports. I hated that he lacked loving emotion. I loved that he brought me to Tahoe for the Winter Olympics. I despised that he always stole the limelight and never listened. The good, the bad, and the ugly feelings were swirling like a cesspool in my mind.

My brother, decked out in a black suit, and I, in a navy blue skirt and jacket, took seats in the front row. Barbara was already seated across the aisle from us with her small white Bichon Frisé, who sat in her lap like he was the one delivering the eulogy.

When it was my turn to speak, I rose, knees trembling like gelatin, and slowly walked toward the casket. There were about thirty people in the room, but I only recognized a few. Willing myself the strength to deliver the eulogy, I attempted to begin several times, but the words lodged in my throat. How could I talk about the father who had broken my heart more times than I cared to remember? I felt so betrayed by him. Caught up in his own life, he never realized he had deprived me of truly knowing and loving him.

Finally, the words tumbled out of my mouth, followed by the sea of emotion I'd been holding back. My voice quivered with every few words and my breathing was shallow. Then, I understood this significant moment was actually a gift, an opportunity for me to heal with my father. Closing my brief tribute, I emphasized how much my daughter would miss the chance to spend more time with her grandfather. With shaking hands and an unsteady emotional voice, I said, "Mariah will always remember her Poppy. The last time he visited, she was Cinderella, in her beautiful blue gown, and he was on one knee playing her Prince Charming." My voice faded and nothing else would come out.

I had decided not to bring my daughter to the funeral, feeling it was unfitting with the family turmoil. Little did I know how right I would be. Young Cinderella would have fond memories of her Prince Charming alive and loving. I can still see her determined look and hear the adamant tone in her voice at Disneyland as she said, "Mommy, I must have the blue dress." How had my daughter known? On some level, she had insight. She had a sixth sense. When I survived the DC-10 plane accident, my assignment was to have a daughter late in life who would be a leader. Had her destiny been cast before she was born? Was my role in life to help her achieve her purpose?

After the funeral, when almost everyone else had left, I stood in the back of the room, away from the casket, with Doug and Barbara. Our stepmother turned to Doug and me and stated, "Your father will rest in peace now. You know there is no will and everything goes to me." Doug and I said nothing, nor did we show any emotions that we knew she was not telling the truth. She went on without missing a beat, training her eyes on me, "I have decided to give Mariah the guest register from today."

Fumbling to say something, my voice cracked, "The register?"

"Yes, the sign-in book of who came to the funeral."

Dumbfounded, I managed to mumble, "That is what you are giving his granddaughter?"

She bobbed her head as she pinched her lips.

Once outside in the parking lot, I glared at Doug and quietly grumbled, "You and I know there is a will. You have a copy and I have one."

Doug shook his head slightly. He fiddled with his dark upscale suit jacket and loosened his pinstripe tie. He appeared to me as if he were being suffocated. Sweat beads formed on his forehead. "Don't worry. I have an appointment with the attorney who drew up the will, and he told me he has the original. According to the copy Father gave me, I am the designated executor," my brother voiced.

I blocked the sun from my eyes with my hand and said, "Father didn't use his usual lawyer, but another one, didn't he? If I remember correctly, the copy of the will I have was drawn up from an attorney I had never heard of before"

My brother agreed.

"He knew this would happen," I went on. "He left us to deal with the wife. He didn't want a confrontation with his own wife when he was alive. He understood she didn't want you and me to inherit anything. To protect us, he went to a new attorney and drew up a will nine years ago. This document had a clear division of assets; we would inherit the business and she would retain the houses and everything else. Nothing is easy with him. When we were younger and he sued for custody, we had to endure court battles. Déjà vu."

"Let's only deal with this issue—I don't want to rehash the past." My brother pulled his keys from his pocket and scanned the parking lot for his car. "I'll meet with the attorney tomorrow. Father told me specifically not to enact the will until the day after his funeral. I have a copy of it and I will take action in the morning." Doug made it sound like this would be a slam-dunk deal — he would handle it, yet my gut was telling me the opposite. War was on the horizon.

Frustrated and standing in the middle of the funeral home parking lot, sweating in the blazing hot sun, I took off my jacket and stressed, "This is not going to be easy. His wife wants everything."

"She gets the two homes, bank accounts, and his investments, but the business, personal belongings, and car will be sold and split between you and me. No matter what she thinks, that is what's written in the will. Those are his wishes and I am determined to fulfill them," Doug emphasized in a stern tone.

Relief washed over me that my brother was dealing with this. I was just too emotional. He would cross all his t's and dot his i's and make sure it was done according to the will. Heaven knows I did not want any more encounters with the stepmother.

"He always asked us not to upset his wife. I have no doubt this is going to upset her, more likely, piss her off. She is convinced she gets it all." Recalling his wishes, I continued, "He wants to be buried in Pennsylvania in the family plot next to his mother and father. Will he be flown back there?"

"According to Barbara, that's all been arranged. She's going to fly back with the casket."

I insisted, "Call me after you meet with the attorney tomorrow. I pray my gut feeling is wrong and we aren't heading into a war."

The next afternoon, the phone rang and Doug said in an irritated tone, "Yes, there is a will; it was written nine years before Father's death and it is valid. I was named executor. Called Barbara and I informed her."

My insides were churning as I groaned. "Let me guess, she was not happy."

"The news of the valid will was…not welcome at all. In fact, she will not be flying to Pennsylvania for the burial, and you and I will have to arrange for the body to be flown back and pay the expenses."

After a couple seconds of silence, Doug finally asked, "Are you there?"

Clearing my throat, I said, "Why didn't Father protect us more?" My intuition was working overtime, and I had a nauseating sensation I couldn't shake. Battle, battle—the word echoed in my brain.

"Don't worry, I'll handle this. There is a conflict of interest with Father's lawyer, so I have already retained a new attorney. The appropriate papers will be filed with the court," he said, sounding very cut-and-dry.

The battle lines had been drawn in the sand, and my fears became reality when the widow hired one of the most aggressive law firms in Reno to contest the will.

The dispute came to life with a vigorous pace. Doug was talking to his attorney every day and appearing in court twice a week, commuting from his home in San Francisco to Reno. We were both buried under mounds of paperwork. It wasn't unusual for the fax machine to be humming out thirty pages at a time or for the FedEx truck to pull up three times a week with thick envelopes containing legal documents. I attempted to keep up with the reading, but understanding the legal terminology was overwhelming. Too much was happening and I had to postpone another trip to visit my mother. No July visit and now the August trip was cancelled. I missed my mom and yearned to be with her. We were healing and I cherished the time we spent together. Why couldn't I be with my mom instead of managing this legal garbage?

There was no time to grieve for a soul who had passed. To look back and understand the lessons learned. To heal with a loved one and move forward with my life. Each day was filled with drama and negative energy flying in my brother's and my directions. No time to enjoy Tahoe…hike a trail, walk on the beach, or laugh with my daughter.

Just when I thought matters couldn't get worse, my close girlfriend and associate lost her battle with cancer and passed away, not even two months after my father died. Lovely Linda, with her blonde hair, smiling face, and wonderfully wicked sense of humor had run my office for years. Linda did more than run my office; she organized my life. She knew everything about me. I couldn't believe she was gone. *I should have spent more time with her. Why didn't I? Because I had trips to the nursing home, I was busy raising my daughter, trying to make a living, and now this crazy legal battle. Forgive me, Linda. You are the best.*

Spend time with your friends

During these months, there was a haze of legal documents and phone calls. Barbara was doing her best to undermine any progress my brother made in running the company. She continued to write checks and spend the company's money on her house payments, remodeling her outdoor deck, car repairs, and gas. My father's business couldn't handle the financial drain. Doug was still not the full executor of the will; his hands were tied by her lawyers' maneuvers. On paper he had the title of executor, but in real life it was another story.

You can't plan, schedule, or demand it; healing happens where and when the time is right. The healing began between my brother and me at a fast food restaurant.

"We're losing. The team of lawyers she retained is blowing my attorney away," my brother lamented.

I said nothing. What could I say? We ate in silence, but I lost my appetite and pushed my salad aside after three bites, sipping on my lemonade without tasting it. My brother's hamburger was only half eaten 'til he shoved it to his left.

He continued, "My attorney is not strong enough for her counsel. I need someone who specializes in business law. You also need a lawyer."

"Me? What kind?"

"A probate lawyer."

"Money, there is an issue called money. I don't have any extra cash to hire a first-rate lawyer. You know with the trips back home, raising my daughter, and not working as much as I'd like, money has been tight."

"They will take the case on a retainer. We pay when we win."

Quickly I shot back, "Reality check! What if we don't win? We still have to pay."

He gave me that look he used to give me when we were kids—the "are you finished with your monologue, drama queen?" look. I sensed his frustration. Maybe we were closer than I thought.

I swatted the air with my hand. "Fine. You have done so much already. Let me see about the attorneys. I live closer to Reno; I'll make some calls and find the right representation." As I said that, my head nodded, but the truth was I didn't know any attorneys. Leaning forward, I clasped my hands. "Here's the deal. You and I will never argue about money. I know we've had our differences, but now we have to be on the same side. The only way we are going to defend ourselves against the opposition is to be united. We only want what is stated in the will."

Too exhausted to talk, he shook his head in agreement.

Sounding confident when I spoke to my brother was one thing, but back in my house with only my daughter and the cat, my fears skyrocketed. My feelings were raw. *Father, are you listening? I am trying not to be angry, but to put us in this position is unfair. You were not man enough to stand up to your wife when you were alive. Now we have to handle this mess. The time, the money, and the stress! I want to be with my daughter, not in some courtroom! Doug has only been married a few months and I am sure he wants to be with his wife instead of dealing with this garbage. You better hang around and help us. You have unfinished business here. Do you hear me? You stick around 'til this entire thing is straightened out, and for God's sake, guide us in making the correct decisions to honor your wishes.*

"Mommy! Mommy! Wake up! Why are you sleeping? Cartoons are over and I'm hungry." I opened my right eye to see a blur of my daughter's face pressed up against mine.

Pulling back a little to let my eyes focus, I choked out, "Well, good morning, Miss Tulip." Glancing over my daughter, I read the digital clock. 9:55.

Giggling, she poked at my face. "Your face is red. Why?" Such innocence.

"Oh, I must have slept on that side of my face."

She stared at me.

Then she laughed, rolling over to snuggle with Sheba, who was occupying half my pillow and still under the assumption that she could continue to sleep peacefully.

"How do pancakes sound for breakfast?"

"Yummy! Yeah, pancakes," Mariah shouted as she tortured the cat to wake up.

"Do you want to go to the pool later? It might be one of the last days to swim before it closes for the season."

Mariah sat straight up. "Swimming! I love the pool." Hopping off the bed, she went skipping down the hall. I watched as she opened her bottom drawer and articles of clothing went flying. "Yeah! I found it." Off went her pajamas and on went her lion bathing suit.

Sitting by the pool was exactly what my soul craved, time to sort out the jumbled thoughts that were racing around my brain. Lawyer, I needed a lawyer who could battle the widow's team. Hell, I needed two lawyers, one for me, and one for my brother. *Where am I going to find a qualified probate and business tax attorneys in a hurry?*

"Watch me. Watch me. I am kicking my feet. I can kick good."

"I see you. Great."

"Mommy, I have a new friend to swim with," Mariah yelled.

I waved as she splashed in the water with a boy around her age.

"Looks like our kids are having a great time," said a striking blonde lady with a slight tan who sat down near me. "I'm Lynne and that's my son, Conner."

"Hi, I'm Donna and that's my daughter, Mariah. When a pool is involved, kids play for hours."

As we chatted, eventually I told her my legal woes. She listened attentively, asking a slew of questions. I told her I needed two attorneys. And, like, yesterday.

After talking for quite a while, as our kids splashed away, she proclaimed. "I am an attorney from Reno."

"You didn't say anything."

She smiled. "You never asked. You know attorneys; we never offer more information than we have to." Her smile broadened. "I wanted to hear the details. Now, I can recommend who you should call to help you with your case." Lynne wrote down the information. "It's not me, but these two attorneys specialize in what you need."

Life is stranger than fiction. What are the chances I would go my homeowner's pool and be referred to an attorney? What made me tell this stranger my woes? Intuition? Does honesty overcome deceit? I sure hoped so.

Lesson Learned:

Focus on a positive outcome

Charter Eleven

Murphy's Law

The receptionist at the law firm answered the phone and quickly asked me to hold. The longer the sound of soothing Beethoven played, the more anxious I became.

Suddenly I heard a pleasant, businesslike voice say, "Donna, this is Janet Crane. Let's briefly discuss what's happening with your case."

After ten minutes of talking, I was impressed by her savvy. She was a probate genius and, I had the feeling, no wimp when it came to courtroom strategies. A chill ran through me when she said, "I want to prepare you. I handle complicated probate cases and yours has all the elements to drag on for years. Win or lose, this case could be very expensive. Even after I review all the material, and if I decide to take the case, I can't guarantee you'll win. By the way, I know Matthew Connolly, whom your brother hired. I have the utmost respect for him as a business tax attorney and his firm."

Her straightforward approach was refreshing. Actually, I felt better after our conversation than I had since the death of my father.

By the following week, both attorneys had reviewed the documents and decided to represent us, and Doug, Matthew, Janet, and I met for an intense two-hour session.

Janet had an air of confidence about her when she spoke. Her flaxen hair had a bounce to it, and with her slim figure, anything she wore looked incredible. She was on the tall side, a height I had wished for my entire life.

"Paperwork and frivolous legal expenses could drain the estate until there is nothing left. We have to reign in your stepmother's representation," my attorney warned.

"His widow is going to use any method she can to make sure Doug and I don't get a dime. She'll do whatever it takes to make that happen, legal or not," I insisted in an acid tone.

The attorneys glanced at each other and then mine spoke. "Let me clarify our position as attorneys. We're going to work diligently to make sure you and Doug receive what's rightfully yours, but we're going to follow the rules and adhere to the law. We don't care if the other side decides to pursue illegal means." She paused for effect and to make sure my brother and I understood her point. "We will abide by the legal system."

By the time the meeting ended, we weren't overly hopeful, but at least we had a greater understanding of Father's will. It all boiled down to the other side refusing to recognize that the business was officially willed to his children.

"We're going to have exorbitant legal bills, how are we going to pay them?" I questioned after we left the law firm.

Doug replied, "When probate is finished, we pay. Our focus is to receive what has been willed to us."

"I guess I'm naïve, since I believed if you wrote a valid will, your wishes would be carried out."

He shook his head. "That's what I thought too. Not in this case."

There were not enough hours in a day to handle the paperwork from the court battle, and my dwindling bank account reminded me that my business was suffering and I had to get back on track. Work became my priority. As if on cue, a client called and booked me for a speaking gig. It was nearing the end of September and I would be off to Denver in a day to give a presentation for a construction association. The late-notice booking was unusual, but I was grateful for the work.

After the airplane leveled off from the turbulent ride over the Sierra Mountains, I settled back in my seat. Elated at the thought of presenting on stage again, I was relieved to be away from the ugly negativity surrounding the court case.

Mr. Wise Man, my mentor, had spent the majority of his time in Denver consulting with people, and I occasionally met him for lunch or dinner if I was in town. I wondered if he had heard my calls to him for help and if he were watching this chaos from another dimension? Being so preoccupied, it had been difficult lately for me to continue my practice of meditation, and I hadn't written in my journal for months. George had clearly stated repeatedly that if I relaxed and said his name and asked for help, he would assist me from the other side.

I glanced around and saw that no one was watching me. I changed positions in my seat to become comfortable, but nothing seemed to soothe me. I crossed my arms, uncrossed them, and adjusted my seat back only to sit it upright again. I closed my eyes and attempted to block out the roar of the engine. My emotions were out of control.

George, I thought, *help! Can you hear me, George? By the way, where exactly are you? Okay, let me get back on track. You know me; I always have a few extra questions. I'm experiencing…so much fear.* My eyes popped wide open like a spectator watching a horror movie. I forced them closed again. *I've never been through anything like this before. My father has passed on and I didn't heal with him. I wanted to and I did talk to him before he passed, but it feels unresolved. I have anger toward my father. I haven't forgiven him for how he treated me in my childhood, and now my brother and I are in this insane probate battle. It's unfair. He is dead and he is still causing me pain. My mother is fighting to stay alive in a nursing home. I want to spend more time with her. I'm raising Mariah, overseeing my business, and meeting with my attorney. I'm* slipping, George. I feel like I'm being drawn into a deep, dark pit. I know there is a spiritual lesson here, but what is it?

I sat in silence as time eluded me. Is my father with you? This is crazy, because I don't have a clue where you are. Give me a sign, George. Please. Now.

More time passed and I focused on staying present in this meditative state, despite the sounds of the flight attendant taking drink orders a few rows up. If you are not going to give me a sign, Mr. Sage Man, will you deliver a message? Would you tell my father I need his help to straighten out this mess? What should my brother and I do to end this fiasco? Stay close, George... I know you said I would get strong in this lifetime and be able to communicate with you, but I don't feel confident. I am losing my will to swim upstream and against the current. It's too difficult. My soul is being sucked from me. I rubbed my temples with a thumb and a spread index finger.

At the Denver Airport I boarded a shuttle to my hotel. When the driver pulled into the circular driveway, I said out loud to no one in particular, "No way!" I quickly scrambled through my briefcase and checked the address. Why hadn't it dawned on me before? It was an Embassy Suites and there must be at least a half-dozen of them in the Denver area, but it was definitely the same hotel. What are the chances?

The last time I was in Denver I stayed at this very hotel and George and I had dinner at the festive Mexican restaurant next door. How George loved his south-of-the-border food with a margarita. He had heard all my woes about an ex-boyfriend dumping me for a young hot number and charging me a fortune to remove him from the deed to my house. Afterwards, we strolled along a path that followed a stream, and George communed with the birds and rabbits, puffing away on his pipe all the time. His telepathic level was so advanced he could communicate with the animals. Mr. Oklahoma Man was a simple but complex soul with an extraordinary gift.

Early the next morning, George had sipped his coffee and gave me a knowing glance. "Donna, I won't always be here. What I'm going to say now, I want you to remember. When you need me, get real still, say my name, and ask for help."

Suddenly my reverie was interrupted by the young woman behind the check-in counter. "May I help you?" I didn't answer until she repeated it louder. "May I help you?"

"I've stayed here before," I said, sounding a bit confused, "but I can't for the life of me recall where the buffet is."

A tall man wearing a manager's badge came out of his office smiling and nodded in my direction. "Sorry to interrupt, but I overheard what you asked. We serve breakfast in the back of the lobby starting at 6 AM." He turned to move away and then abruptly changed his mind. "Also, there is a great shopping mall across the street where you can find restaurants, clothing stores, and, if you're interested, a famous tobacco shop."

At first I could only gawk at him. *A tobacco shop?* Slowly I said, "Thank you," and watched the manger return to his office.

Leaning closer to the clerk, I asked, "Does he smoke?"

"Actually, no," she stated.

Riding the glass elevator, I thought about my mentor. *George, you are around me? Right! This seems so like you. You and your blooming pipe tobacco. Always had to have that unique blend. It is you, I am sure of it. I sense you. I was probably too uptight on the airplane and you couldn't telepathically reach me. Leave it to me, I was blocking you. Sorry. You told me again and again to relax, get calm. Not my normal personality, but you know that. I wasn't thinking about you when I arrived at the hotel and wow, you showed up. Thanks, George, sure miss seeing your smiling face*

Exiting the elevator on the third floor, I wheeled my luggage down the hall. Peering around, I felt a flutter of familiarity; I had traveled this path before. I paused before the door leading into my corner room to verify I had the correct number. Could it be the same room? I checked the number again, third floor and the corner room. Stranger things have happened. I unlocked the door and stepped inside. It was the exact room I had stayed in on my last visit. *A coincidence, I didn't think so. George, you are here! My girlfriend, Jeanne, in Denver, I need to call her. She will understand.*

George had introduced us in 1979, and it wasn't odd that Jeanne and I had remained friends over the years. George told me he had been assigned twelve souls to guide on this Earth, and Jeanne and I were the only females. Of course it took him years to tell me that bit of information, because he would only divulge insight if the timing was right and if the soul was ready to handle the knowledge.

Calling my girlfriend, I quickly blurted out, "I think George is around me! No. I take that back. I know George is around me."

She didn't miss a beat. "Why? What happened?"

"I asked him for his help while I was flying here today. Nothing happened, but when I checked in at the hotel, it turned out to be the same hotel I stayed in when I last visited George. I'm in exact room I stayed in before. The manager told me about the mall next door and a tobacco shop."

"That's the shop where I bought George's cherry pipe tobacco," Jeanne said, sounding surprised. "It was a special blend, and the owner had to order it for me. George had to have that certain blend and no other tobacco would do. I'm jumping in the car and coming right over. We'll have an early dinner and talk."

George! George, you never fail to surprise me. You have an odd way of letting me know you are around. Glad to see you haven't lost your humor. Of course, I'm not sure how you made all those coincidences occur.

At dinner we were on overdrive when it came to our conversation; there was so much to share. Jeanne's upbeat attitude was contagious, and that is what I craved.

"Do you remember that first time you came to Denver and shopped in my clothing store?" Jeanne asked.

Laughing, I confirmed, "Oh yeah, still have the green suede dress I bought. Quality stuff." In a more serious tone, I said, "Sure miss that Mr. Miracle Worker and his Georgeisms. I use to hate them, but now I understand the wisdom of his little parables."

"George would say to me, 'Are you gonna fish or cut bait?' He wanted me to make a decision and not be so wishy-washy." Jeanne shook her head and grinned, her sparkly earrings flashing alluringly in the cozy restaurant lighting.

"Yeah, with me he would say, 'Can't expect a first-grader to do twelfth-grade homework.' Oh boy, I detested that one, but George wouldn't budge. He insisted if a person wasn't mature or spiritual, they were not capable of doing advanced work yet and it would take time."

Jeanne's grin turned soft as she stared at the wedge of lemon in her water glass. "This is like rummaging through my brain. Funny how his Georgeisms pop up."

Window-shopping was next on the agenda. We strolled over the bridge to the shopping mall of little boutiques, with upscale clothing, pottery, and even a very unique stationary store. Trees and massive plants were everywhere in this covered mall, and scattered around were wooden benches. Abruptly, both of us stopped and stared. Before us was the tobacco shop.

"Let's go in," Jeanne said with enthusiasm. "I used to come to this shop all the time to pick up George's special blend of pipe tobacco."

The shop's owner recognized her right away. How could anyone not remember Jeanne, a striking, tall brunette with a larger-than-life personality? "Well, isn't this a nice surprise. I haven't seen you in a long time. Where have you been keeping yourself?" the heavyset owner with a slight accent and a receding hair line asked.

She told him about George's passing.

The shopkeeper shook his head slowly. "He was a remarkable man, and kind. Always had something nice to say about the human race." He appeared deep in thought and then unexpectedly he explained, "I still have a bag of George's cherry tobacco in back. It's such a special blend; I couldn't sell it to anyone else. I'll give it to you. On the house."

Jeanne glanced at me and then turned to the owner. "That is very kind of you."

"Quite all right."

"Could I ask you a favor?" Jeanne said with a smile.

"Sure," the owner stated.

"Could you divide the tobacco into two bags for us?"

"My pleasure."

When he returned with two neatly sealed plastic bags, I couldn't help but chuckle. Here I was, a non-smoker, clutching a bag of cherry tobacco like it was the finest Belgian chocolate. Holding the bag rekindled fond memories of the smell of George's pipe, a signature scent to anyone who knew him.

We burst into laughter after we left the shop. Finally catching my breath, I said, "Mr. Miracle Man is around us sending a loud message like a megaphone announcement, or this is a gigantic coincidence!" I continued, "George, keep checking in with me, because the battle over my father's estate is heating up. Could use some major support. "

Lesson Learned:

Be open to unexpected help

Chapter Twelve

It's Not about the Money

It was a crisp and brilliantly clear day at Lake Tahoe, but I was stuck inside the house with three bulky FedEx envelopes facing me. The thought of opening them and having to deal with their contents caused me to be apprehensive and on the verge of tears. My brother and I talked constantly, but instead of achieving positive results, our case was bogged down with glitches and delays. Each hitch cost more energy and money.

I was frozen in time, staring at my computer screen. Feeling too weighed down, I didn't have the capacity to focus, to work. Being with my daughter would be more rewarding, but Mariah was at the park with Sara. *Get out of this state. It is not doing you any good. You have to work. Concentrate!*

Continuing to gape at my screensaver, the thought occurred to waste more time and look for a new picture; maybe a kitten, a puppy, or a butterfly that would cheer me up and make me feel like my old self. Clicking through pages of pictures, I noticed a lotus flower. *Nice but... what?* My search continued fruitlessly, so I started scrolling backwards, stopping when I saw the lotus flower again. There was something about it that intrigued me.

During an internet search for the significance of a lotus flower, I read it was a symbol of spiritual awakening. The magnificent lotus emerges from the dirty and murky bottom of a pond and yet remains untouched by all the dirt and mud of the environment. Though the flower has its roots in the mud, it grows upward toward the light. Quickly changing my screensaver to the brilliant lotus, while speaking to the splendid image, I said, "Beautiful flower, will you be my reminder? I need to rise above this negativity and understand the lesson I must learn." Chuckling, I realized I was talking to a screensaver. I also talked to my cat, not to mention the times I communicated with George, who had died years ago... And I thought my life was boring. Looking at the magnificent lotus image, I felt a sense of peace. "Thank you, flower, I am now ready to get back to work."

Pulling into my driveway two days later, I blinked at a miraculous sight. Well, an extraordinary sight to me: my father's dark and sleek sports car parked in my driveway. The car was willed to my brother and me, but had been "mysteriously" missing every time Doug claimed it in court. Doug first requested the car in July and it was now September 30th. Dashing into the house, I saw the nanny, kissed my daughter, patted the cat, and there on the kitchen table was the paperwork for the car and the keys.

"A guy dropped it off and left," Sara said, shrugging her shoulders.

Shouting into the phone at my brother, I uttered, "How did we get the car?"

"There is good news and bad news. The car is the trophy for winning our first battle. It was awarded to you, because as the executor, I could not take it due to a conflict of interest. You sell it and put the money in the estate bank account."

"I have to sell the car? Now?"

"Right, but hang on. Here is the other news," Doug said, annoyed.

"What?"

"Barbara's attorney has filed a motion to throw out father's will on the grounds he wasn't of sound mind at the time it was written. Bottom line, they're contesting the will."

"That's ridiculous. Father worked and ran a business for nine years after he wrote his will. How can they say he was nuts?"

"I don't know, but her side is trying to do just that. I have to hang up, my business line is ringing."

I slowly cradled the phone and then picked it up again to call Janet.

She had hardly said hello when I blasted out my question. "How can she say my father was crazy and the will is invalid?"

"Calm down, this is pretty typical and one of the ways the other side can contest the will. I do not doubt the state of your father's competency, but this can take months to resolve. It's a delay tactic. I am meeting with your brother's attorney tomorrow morning and we will decide what strategy to pursue," Janet said firmly.

Why did it seem we were going one step forward and two steps back? *This is insane. How long can this go on? I want my life back.*

Every night was insomnia frenzied as I tossed and turned. Running on adrenaline for months, my mind was too troubled to rest during this ugly fight. Countless emotions surged through me: love, hate, anger, betrayal.

My head throbbing, I threw back the covers and grabbed my robe. The dark, silent house felt chilly. Storming to the living room, I glared out the window to see the reflection from Father's sleek new car. The glossy green automobile was bathed in the glow of a streetlight. Restless and unsettled, I felt trapped in an endless court battle.

With a rush of emotion, I jerked open the front door. Cold air whirled around my body as I heard the rustle of leaves. Anger welled up as I screamed, "You loved your cars more than you loved me. You always had to have a new one. Telling me about your fancy automobiles was always more important than what was happening in my world." I didn't care if anyone heard me as my fury boiled. Circling the car, I peered inside at the plush interior while picturing him driving his latest prize, his status car.

My hands balled into fists as I struck the hood. Again and again I attacked the car, unleashing years of rage and resentment, cursing, "Damn you, Father."

Finally falling to my knees, I wept uncontrollably, incoherent garble spilling from my mouth. "How...how could you! How could leave us in this...this mess?"

Tears streaming down my face, I stared up at the ebony sky embellished with blazing stars. I was oozing bitterness. *For years you dragged me and Doug to court for custody. We were only kids! God forgive you. You're dead and doing it to us again. Answer me, why?*

Curling into a fetal position on the cold asphalt, near the front tire, the adrenaline finally drained out of me. I sucked oxygen back into my lungs and let it out. I kept gulping breaths until the crushing weight of anger slowly started to subside.

At first, the words I heard resounding in my head were obscured, but as I grew calmer, they became more coherent. *I'm sorry. I am so sorry. I am here to help.*

Afraid to move, I shivered. Could it be? Was my father here? George taught me to ask for help and trust the answer. He insisted I shouldn't intellectualize the thought, but rather honor the message and know that it was the truth, even if it was a fleeting insight.

Lesson Learned:

Healing happens when the time is right

Chapter Thirteen
Here We Go Again

Frosty December arrived in a flurry of blustery snowstorms. Months of court battles and an extended trip to Pennsylvania to visit my mother left me physically and emotionally exhausted. To maintain some sanity, but mostly to get Mariah excited for the holidays, I climbed up the ladder to string Christmas lights on the eaves. Soft white snowflakes fell on my face and quickly melted. I was thankful for a normal day until the FedEx guy showed up.

"Hey, Ben, how are you?" I yelled from the ladder as I hooked up another string of lights. "You're not bringing me more nasty legal muck to wreck my holiday mood, are you?"

Ben smiled while pretending to hide the package behind his back. "Don't shoot the messenger! Sorry, this is a big one. Have a happy holiday."

At first I wanted to ignore the package, but it dared me to open it. Attaching the last line of lights into place, I climbed down the ladder, tore open the envelope, and extracted the hefty sheaf. There, on the first page, it said that Father's office manager, an outspoken advocate for the other side, had given notice.

My brother had relayed to me that the office manager had been making it difficult for him to run the company. He was also aware that she communicated with Barbara on a regular basis. She was older and I could only imagine the stress that must have been wearing on her. Since there was so much turmoil and drama at the office every day, perhaps she realized there was no solution in sight and that was why she had quit.

I read on to find that our stepmother had jumped ahead and appointed a manager to fill the position, since she claimed she was an owner in the business.

Leaving the ladder and leftover lights in the driveway, I dashed in the house to call my brother. The business taxes were filed as sole ownership under my father's name. I assumed that Doug's position as executor of the estate gave him the right to approve or disapprove the new manager.

"I'm reading my copy now," Doug said. His sharp tone told me he was irate trying to figure out yet another legal document. "It takes a while to get through thirty pages of double-talk."

"Do you even understand what it says?"

"Somewhat. If you cut to the chase, her attorney says they are going to take over the office this coming Friday unless we hire a manager before that time."

My throat tightened. "We only have three days to hire someone? Where are we going to find a person qualified so quickly?" Weak-kneed, I dropped down on the sofa, fighting back tears. "It's impossible. It's almost Christmas! Who is looking for work and will start by Friday, this week? They've backed us into a corner," I wailed.

"Hold it. Give me a minute to think."

As I waited, staring mournfully out the window at the white sparkling lights, I searched my thoughts. *Help! Help! Please! We need a solution! Please...* Abruptly, an intuitive flash interrupted my begging. *Could it be? Could it work?* Standing upright, I announced, "I think I've come up with something."

"Let's have it," Doug demanded.

"There's a job placement agency in Reno, ProNet, that specializes in administrative managers and executives. They're clients of mine. I've done training seminars for their members."

"Call them right now. Let me know if they have someone we can hire."

My conversation with the agency representative was brief and to the point. Within minutes of hanging up, resumes began pouring from my fax machine. I sorted through the pile and called my brother.

Sounding relieved, he commanded, "You arrange the interviews and I'll drive up there. We should meet at Father's business accountant's office to make sure nothing is amiss. We can even ask their office manager to sit in on the interviews. We might just pull this off," Doug stated hopefully.

The next day, we interviewed six people and decided our top candidate was a qualified woman, Darlene, who had managed a medical office. We tendered an offer and informed her she would have to start the next day. Her eyes blinked rapidly, though she maintained her composure, uttering pleasantly, "Okay. I can do that."

My brother explained, "Great. We are glad to have you. There might not be extensive training from the manager who is leaving, because she will only be in the office for one more day. I will be by your side to help you get started."

"All right. Give me some time and I know I'll learn the ropes. I'll be at the office at 8 AM tomorrow."

She arrived punctually at headquarters the next morning and dove straight into the job. Her learning curve was vertical and she had to be frustrated, but she never let it show.

We weren't too surprised to hear from our attorneys that our victory was greeted with a vicious retort. The following Monday, my brother was slapped with a summons to appear in court. Our stepmother's attorney had fired another volley and filed against us, stating we were not qualified to hire a manager for the business. I was furious as I read the papers, which claimed that since I had never worked in the background communication field and did not manage a staff, I should not have been party to the decision-making process of hiring the new office manager.

Within two days, Doug was in the courtroom facing the judge, his attorney by his side. After reviewing all the pertinent information, the judge ruled our choice competent to fill the position of office manager and that Doug had acted appropriately as the executor. My brother called after he left the courtroom, informing me that we had missed another bullet.

Later that night, I fell into bed, shattered and exhausted. Everything in this ordeal with Barbara was happening at such warp speed that there was little time to process before reacting to each new allegation. The fatigue was devastating.

Moments later I heard, "Mommy. Mommy! Can I come snuggle with you and Sheba? I miss you." Her soft voice echoed as she stood at my door.

"Mariah, jump right in beside me," I said in a sleepy tone.

"Yeah!" She tumbled on the bed, dragging her pink blanket and four stuffed animals.

Turning to Sheba, I giggled. "You better move over. I don't know if there is room for you and all these animals."

"Mommy, I have been a very good girl."

Watching my daughter's eyes and realizing it was only a week 'til Christmas, I was starting to figure out what she was saying. "Are you telling me this so I will deliver the message to Santa Claus?" Mariah beamed as her little head bobbed up and down. "Got it," I said. "You are a great kid and Santa will be informed."

Mariah snuggled closer, falling asleep on my pillow. Sheba raised her head, staring at me as if to say, *Can I get some sleep now?*

I kissed them both and grinned. My life was not traditional, but it was my life and I would have to learn how to keep it together. Healing is not grandiose, but little steps and little moments. The ugliness I was facing on a daily basis was disheartening, but when I came home to my daughter and cat, I felt wanted.

Lesson Learned:

Truth and integrity prevail

Chapter Fourteen

Academy Award Performance

Chocolate chip cookies are a holiday tradition. With only four days 'til the church bells would ring, ushering in Christmas, Mariah and I were hard at work in the kitchen. "Here, Mariah, roll the dough into little balls in your hands and place them about two inches apart. Like this."

"I love cookies," Mariah sang as she danced around the kitchen, licking cookie dough off her fingers. "Cookies are yummy. Can we make some for Aunt Donna and Uncle Dougie? Please! Can we?"

"That's very thoughtful. Aunt Donna is visiting her family in Virginia and Uncle Dougie is traveling to Pennsylvania to visit Nana in the nursing home."

"Oh."

"There goes the doorbell. I'll get it. You can watch the cookies."

"Yes, I will watch the cookies!"

I chuckled, knowing that as soon as I left the kitchen she would attack the dough.

On my doorstep was yet another FedEx package. I reached for it, hesitating, as a hint of forewarning tingled through me. I ripped into it and began to read. My jaw dropped open. An emergency board meeting had been called for nine o'clock the next morning. *Oh, my God. How could Barbara do this?* My thoughts flew back to a discussion I'd had with Doug about the operations of our father's business. The powerful receiving tower used to broadcast the music to the clients was retained as an asset of a small corporation. This was held separate from the business, which was a sole proprietorship. The reason for this was to keep the tower operating if the business shut down. My father had listed me as one of the directors on the inactive board of the tower corporation along with his wife, two other people, and himself.

Skimming through the next few documents, it became obvious that our stepmother had reached out to the other two directors, activated the board, and was now set to shut down the tower. I wasn't as well-versed in the business as my brother, but I knew this: no tower…no business.

A surge of panic clenched my chest. My first impulse was to call Doug, but he was en- route to Pennsylvania. Grabbing a copy of his flight schedule, I saw that I would not reach him until after 10 PM. Barbara knew my brother wouldn't be in town. Doug had given Father's old office manager his itinerary a week before she resigned.

"Mommy. Mommy." The oven timer rang from the kitchen. "The cookies are ready."

I dropped the offensive package on the table and arranged the freshly baked chocolate chip cookies on a tray to cool and a few on a plate for my daughter. "Wow, you did a fantastic job. They look great. Yum, I bet they taste wonderful," I proclaimed, attempting to inflate myself with some positive energy.

"Can I eat mine now?"

"Sure, let me pour some milk. Put the cookies on your table and when you are finished you can play. I have to read some papers. We will make some more cookies later."

"Okay," she said, already eyeing the treats.

Sitting at the kitchen table, I reviewed the package. I was sure Barbara had deliberately planned the meeting for when my brother would be out of town. Could it be she was actually trying to destroy the company to prevent us from owing it? Insanity on her part.

I gazed outside as snow began to fall, sprinkling the landscape with fresh winter powder. After a minute or so, the wind whipped and the flurries gained in intensity, enveloping my view in swirling white. The weather was mimicking my world; one minute peaceful and the next minute it was out of control.

Commencing my customary pacing through the house, I searched for answers…kitchen, dining, living room, back and forth, a journey to nowhere. Finally slowing down, I paused to take in the heat radiating from the logs burning in the fireplace while gazing into the flames. *Why? Why do I continue to stay in the battle with my stepmother? Why don't I throw in the towel? My brother and I could lose. Why not get out now? Walk away. Is it the money…?* Out loud I said with intensity, "Is it the money?"… *No! No it's more than that. If I walk, I would still have to pay thousands in attorney fees but…it's the principle! Our father honored us by his acknowledgement in his will. Is there a higher purpose in this battle that I must endure and understand this greed? Is it because this is the path to heal the complicated relationship with my father?*

I hastened to the kitchen phone and called my attorney. "I…I got a…"

"Donna, I know. I'm clearing my calendar right now to work on this. We have to prepare. They cannot gain control of the tower, or you and your brother will lose everything. Your stepmother's attorney is trying to outmaneuver us. I'll call you at the end of the day."

All I could think of was how do you stop a bulldozer? Janet sounded so intense. I flopped myself down dramatically onto the couch near my Christmas tree. Mariah was contentedly cutting out white snowflakes from construction paper while she hummed a holiday tune. I yearned to be a child again, distracting myself from the big issues by doing little things. I was sure Mariah's next move would be to hang her new designs on the tree. Taking in the red and silver ornaments, hundreds of red bows and oval white beads gave it a Victorian appearance. *Why couldn't*

I be living at that time instead of now?

Christmas! I should be happy. My memory knew I had experienced worse. A Christmas a few years ago, where I was intentionally snubbed and made to feel unwelcome. I had been invited by my father to spend the day with them, but when I arrived promptly at 2 PM as told, the gifts had already been opened and they had eaten Christmas dinner without me. I was shocked, no, appalled, feeling like I was not a part of this family as I stood in the kitchen picking off small pieces of turkey meat from its carcass. My father tried to start a conversation as I stood there, but I was burning inside and didn't want to talk. I don't think he understood my feelings. It was Christmas day and I was single, yearning for a family more than anything, but after arriving and having been eliminated from the festivities, I felt unbearably alone. As George would have said, "Can't make a square peg fit in a round hole." I didn't feel connected, but I smiled and kept my feelings to myself. The next morning, I had gone to the doctor, needing antibiotics for a case of strep throat. I had felt violated and betrayed, and I had internalized my frustration, which retaliated in the form of sickness.

Now I vowed that I would speak my mind and not be pushed aside during this probate ordeal. I wasn't sure how I would do this, but I knew if I was going to be true to my spirit, that was my path. *Was this a spiritual lesson for me to honor my soul?*

As promised, my attorney called later that afternoon. "I need more time to review the documents before we talk. I'll meet you at 8 AM sharp tomorrow morning at the opposition's office. Don't be late, and don't worry. I'll have a strategy by then."

"Okay," I mumbled, sounding very unsure. "See you in the morning."

When I knew that Doug had arrived in Pennsylvania, I called. I first inquired about Mom's health and then quickly changed the subject to the tower board meeting tomorrow.

My brother came unglued. "For God's sake! We'll go out of business! Do you understand?" he blustered into the phone. "If they shut that tower down, we'll have to close the doors."

"What do you want me to do?"

"You have to stop them!"

My shaky voice didn't even sound like me. "I spoke with my attorney. She's working on a strategy."

"What's her plan?"

The last thing he wanted to hear: "I don't know. I'm meeting with her first thing in the morning. She's professional and aggressive," I pitched in.

"This is our worst nightmare. Handing us Father's car was just a carrot to suck us in deeper. I'm taking the next flight out of here."

I couldn't blame him for overreacting. He'd been through six months of hell. This ordeal started in July; now it was only days from Christmas, and he was about to be outmaneuvered and outsmarted.

"You're back east," I said. "There aren't any flights leaving until morning. You'd never make it in time."

A sigh. "You're right. You know she planned this. She knew I would be out of town. We have only one choice. You have to stop this from happening!"

"Why did Father put me on this limited advisory board anyway?"

Doug snapped, "He wanted to make you feel like you were part of the business. Stop them! Just stop them. Have your attorney do something. Let me know."

That night I desperately tried to put together ideas on how to stop the tower from being closed. But my mind had created a psychological firewall and had canceled out even a gleam of hope at coming up with a concept. I prayed to God, George, my father, and any angels who were listening in. *What am I supposed to do? I don't like confrontation. I don't want to go head-on in a battle, yet here I am about to do it. Why? Why me? There has to be a spiritual purpose. There has to be a reason. What? What is it? George, you always said a person went through difficult, challenging times to make them stronger. It was for their spiritual growth. I hate being forced to be stronger. If*

I get much stronger, I won't need a door—I'll just walk right through the wall.

The next morning, standing in the lobby of the opposing law offices, looking every inch the professional in a crisp designer suit, my attorney motioned me to lean in closer to her and quietly said, "I think I've found a way to stop them, but you'll have to do it."

What do you mean? I'm paying you to represent me to the best of your ability. Why do I have to do it?

Urgency sharpened her words as she said softly, "I have about two minutes to explain this to you."

"I'm listening."

"The lawyer is representing both the business and your stepmother. It's a blatant conflict of interest and it's illegal. It's our trump card. When we go inside, you'll have to have him admit before witnesses that he is representing the business as well as your stepmother. This needs to happen during the board meeting."

Through clenched teeth I muttered, "How am I supposed to do that?"

"You can do it."

"Explain what I have to do!"

My attorney quietly outlined the plan as we walked toward the inner sanctum.

Trembling inside, I sat down at an oval conference table with my stepmother, her lawyer, and the other board members. Janet and I sat on the right side, and Barbara and the other board members were on the left. Barbara's lawyer stood at the head. Though my attorney appeared unmoved, the tension in the room was palpable. *Let me out of here right now. I want out!*

Since that wasn't going to happen, I inhaled deeply and thought, *Let the outcome be for the highest good.*

The widow's attorney, dressed in a distasteful brown suit, which was ill-fitting, with his mouth open, ready for his rehearsed spiel, explained in a cocky tone why we were here, obviously assured that this was going to be a win-win day for his client. He gazed at me with narrowed eyes. Young and full of himself, he was out to make his mark and impress his client with energy that permeated the room, demanding everyone's attention.

During the lawyers' discourse, I heard them declare the existing directors' terms were up and nominations for re-election were in order. The other three board members put their heads together for a powwow and then proceeded to nominate each other. Why wasn't I shocked when no one nominated me?

Thinking fast, I announced, "I nominate myself."

I heard a gasp, then some tongue clucking, and saw a series of scornful expressions that implied I was the cluck.

"Is anyone going to second the nomination?" I asked. Glancing around the impressive mahogany conference table, I could tell no one was going to second the motion. No surprise.

I hadn't the slightest idea how I was going to get her attorney to admit to a conflict of interest. I had heard about him, but this was the first time I was going to interact with him. The nomination was only a stall tactic. *Think Donna. Think, think, think.* My mind raced back to my acting days in Los Angeles. Then it struck me…the character of the bumbling detective, Lieutenant Columbo.

I lowered my head and unhurriedly glanced up, assuming a bewildered look. "Can….can I ask a question? I'm really confused here. I guess I should know more about being on the board and all, but if I have a question about my father's business…" I looked straight at my stepmother's attorney as I tilted my head. "Are you the person who should answer it?"

Arching his back, and with a hint of arrogance in his voice, he stated, "Of course."

"Then…if I have a question pertaining to my stepmother, you know, like her involvement and all, do I ask you? You know, like, in the meeting if I get confused. This is kinda new for me and a lot to take in."

"Yes. You would ask me." He smiled a condescending smile that didn't reach his eyes.

Raising my hand like a child in a classroom, I said while clicking my pen in the other hand, "Hold on a minute. I need to write this down." I smiled at him and wrote on my legal tablet.

He began to pontificate about the receiving tower and who should control it.

"Excuse me!" Up went my hand like a third grader. "I'd like to take notes, but right now I can't understand a thing you're saying. So, to clarify what you said earlier, I can ask you questions about my father's business, the tower, and any other concerns and you'll explain it to me, right?"

He glared at my attorney, with a look that implied incredible impatience—*Can't you control your client from asking such stupid questions?* Janet's face was calm and free of emotion—as usual, the picture of professionalism. Clearing his throat, Barbara's attorney continued, "Yes. I already told you that!"

"Then any questions about Father's house and his safety-deposit box, you could answer those, right?" He stared at me. "Well, sometimes I get all the information mixed up in my mind."

He rolled his eyes upwards. "Yes. Must I put it in writing for you or do you understand now?"

I shrugged. "I kinda think so. Hmm, sorry, I guess not really. I don't understand."

The other board members made muffled, insulting comments, making sure I overheard.

Totally exasperated and in his best attorney posture, our stepmother's lawyer announced, "Let me articulate once more so you understand, Ms. Hartley. Then we must move on. I am representing your father's business. Do you understand that?"

I nodded. "One more question...."

He was so incensed with me, as he raised his voice even louder and hissed. "And I represent Mrs. Hartley!" Glaring at me, he didn't move.

"Got it," I said in a weak fumbling voice. *Thank you, Lieutenant Columbo.* Stealing a quick glance at Janet, I saw a twinkle in her eye. She understood what I was doing.

By the end of the meeting, I was voted off the board, leaving the other members in charge. After a round of hand shaking, with everyone but me and my attorney, the satisfied board members trooped out of the room, talking celebratory lunch, I'm sure at an expensive dining establishment. Outside the conference room, I heard the stepmother's arrogant, offensive attorney announce he would have the paperwork completed within the next twenty-four hours. I knew what that meant... shut down the receiving tower and Father's business. A chill ran up my spine. I wasn't sure what had just occurred. Either I had pulled it off or lost it all.

Janet nudged me. "Hurry. Let's go."

Once we were alone outside, her dazzling smile said it all. "You did it. Though he didn't realize it, her attorney admitted in front of five people that he is in conflict, but he'll know soon. He now has to choose to represent either the business or your stepmother. We've bought some time. I'm going back to my office to draft a letter, messenger it to the court, and stop the tower injunction from getting signed. When I get the order back, I'll messenger a copy to him. You're still in business." Gawking, my mouth was open. "Donna, don't worry, this will buy us time. You did it."

Doug called three times that day. I knew he was anxious when he raised his voice at me on the last phone call when I was in the kitchen preparing dinner with Mariah. My little assistant was washing vegetables while talking, going on and on about a story she had read. A little pony found a new loving home for Christmas, and that made my daughter ecstatic. Why couldn't I be as content as my daughter?

Janet rang right before we sat down to eat, laughing as she said, "I listened to the nastiest message I have ever received and read a one-page letter deliberately implying how he couldn't believe what lowdown, cutthroat, and ruthless tactics I used. He didn't like that he was outsmarted." She cleared her throat. "By the way, I was rushed earlier and didn't get the chance to say how well you did at the board meeting."

It was the first time during the day I felt I could relax as I replied, "I was an actress in Los Angeles. I believe my acting lessons paid for themselves today."

"I would say so. The really good news is, because of the conflict, the court has dismissed the insanity allegation against your father. The court ruled your father was not insane nine years ago when he wrote the will."

Something in the tone of her voice made me ask, "What are you not telling me?"

"Her attorney is so upset, he asked for another court date, insisting that your father's wife is and was an equal business partner and now should inherit half the business. This is in addition to the homes, bank accounts, and insurance that is rightfully hers by way of the will."

"Wait," I said, massaging my temple at the site of an oncoming migraine. I tried to process her words. "Let me understand this. They can't shut down the tower, so we're still in business, and my father was not insane at the time he drafted the will. The will states that my brother and I inherit the business and must sell it and divide the profits, but her side is now claiming that she is a legal business partner and should inherit half the business."

"That's right."

"Will this ever stop?"

"It's the holiday season and not much happens in the courts until after New Year's. We'll set up a meeting January 2nd , including your brother and his attorney. I'll have my secretary call everyone to schedule it."

"Thank you," I said as I felt I was slipping off the end of a diving board with no water below. "Happy holidays."

Escaping to my living room to light up the Christmas tree, I paused to gather my thoughts before calling my brother. My mind in turmoil, my thoughts drifted to my missing mentor, George. *This is some ride I am on. You were adamant that everything happens for a reason. Well, what is the reason? Spiritual…healing…relationships…truth…persistence…trust…*

forgiveness... Whatever it is, why do I have a dreadful feeling the end of this war is nowhere in sight?

Lesson Learned:

Perseverance triumphs

Chapter Fifteen
For Your Highest Good

Dawn had broken through the clouds on an icy Tahoe morning as I backed the car out of the driveway. My Subaru was ten years old and still going strong, handling the treacherous mountain roads without ever failing its driver. My teeth chattered from the frigid cold, but I knew switching on the heater would be worthless until the car had warmed up. It was nearing the end of a blustery January, and I was making my way to the courthouse to meet my brother and our attorneys. Over the past few weeks, Doug and I had spent hours holed up with our lawyers, developing a strategy. By now, I should have had a handle on what binding arbitration meant, but I couldn't imagine our stepmother would consent to anything binding unless it ruled in her favor.

We all exchanged greetings as the four of us trudged up the stone steps leading to the courthouse. A harsh wind whipped at our faces and swept wintry drafts through my coat. But the chill invading my body was more from a looming fear of defeat rather than the weather.

Walking down the hallway, Janet confirmed, "I think you're going to be happy with the judge assigned to your arbitration. I couldn't have hand-selected a more eminent jurist. I want to make sure you and Doug have a thorough understanding of what binding arbitration means."

We looked at her blankly, so Janet continued, sounding like a textbook, "It's the submission of a dispute to an unbiased third person designated by the parties to the controversy, who agree in advance to comply with the final ruling. Which means what the judge rules today is binding to all parties involved." Her gaze was direct. "That includes your stepmother."

I knew Doug and I could live with the outcome. After seven months of absolute hell, the bickering had to stop. But what was there to prevent the other side from finding some kind of loophole? Or, for that matter, to prevent Barbara from scoffing at the ruling? No one could guarantee she would abide by the judge's decision, but I, for one, didn't have the time or the energy to spend on another day of this madness. The thought struck me that the reason for my being here today was because of decisions my father had made. *Father, you had better be here too.*

It wasn't just my imagination that had caused me to think that my father's spirit would be in the courtroom. Last night, and many times before, the light in my daughter's room had turned on spontaneously. It began turning on in the middle of the night, without apparent cause, soon after I threw the late-night hissy fit and attacked my father's car. An important lesson emerged from my tantrum—how pent-up anger can cause you to act crazy. I mean really insane, enough to assault a car. I believe my father got the message that I was fuming and he had better help out...pronto.

At first, when the light went on, I thought Mariah had gotten up after a bad dream and turned it on to feel safe. Losing her Poppy had left my daughter anxious about my mortality, and she would sometimes crawl into bed with me. But it didn't make a difference whether she was in her room or mine. The light would eerily self-activate two or three nights a week. It triggered a notion that my father was contacting me by causing the light to go on. George had told me that loved ones from the other side could contact humans by sending their energy through electricity.

I believed this was his way of telling me he was watching over us as we struggled to find a way to end the nightmare his will had turned into.

Janet laid her briefcase on the conference table and turned to us. "I want to reassure you that the judge is decisive, fair, and has a reputation for his no-nonsense attitude." She paused, and said in a more serious tone, "But you should also keep in mind that there is a chance the ruling may not be in your favor. If I didn't make you aware of that, I would be negligent in not preparing you."

As I listened to my attorney's sage advice, doubt tiptoed in. I took a deep breath, then another, and voiced the concerns that had plagued me. "What if the judge comes up with a viable plan Doug and I can live with, but the widow balks at the very idea? Worse yet, what if the judge gets fed up and decides to stop the arbitration proceedings altogether? Does that mean we have to go to trial?"

My lawyer shot Doug's attorney a glance. "If that happens, the judge will keep her under control. She'll insist she is a partner and entitled to half the business. We do have an advantage. Doug has been working off and on in your father's business since he was a teenager and partnered with him right up until your father died." I started to interrupt, but Janet raised both palms. "Today is not a toss of the dice. We are availing ourselves of every rule and principle the legal system has to offer."

I glanced at Doug.

"I'm pretty apprehensive for all the same reasons you are, but we have to believe in the system," my brother remarked, his shoulders hiked up with tension.

I knew in my heart Doug was right. He was coming from an intellectual viewpoint whereas I viewed everything emotionally.

It is strange to admit, but something good comes of everything. My brother and I had become closer than ever. The stepmother hadn't counted on the fact that we would join forces and have each other's back. We hadn't been this bound by mutual loyalty since we were children. *Hmm, George, are you watching this from wherever you are? My brother and*

I are healing. Maybe not in the conventional way; it's more like, we are in this together, on the same side. I'm understanding there is no formula for healing. My lesson…accept it, in any form it arrives.

The bailiff announced it was time to walk us to the judge's chambers.

George, the time is now. In fact, I need you with me all day. If my father is there with you, bring him along. If you know any good judges or attorneys up there, bring them along too. I chuckled, as I could imagine George saying something like, *Might be a full house in the judge's chambers, but I'll see what I can do.*

Lesson Learned:
Survive the journey

Chapter Sixteen

The Gavel Rules

The judge's chamber was expansive and statelier than I had imagined, with one entire wall dominated by massive windows and an imposing dark oak desk. Our stepmother's entourage included two attorneys—the young lawyer who had maneuvered the takeover of the music tower but who had failed with his grandstanding and almost ruined my Christmas, plus a senior partner from the same firm. Now she had one to represent her on the probate of her husband's will and the other to fight for her ownership in the business.

My stomach churned. I had the sensation of walking into a lion's den, and the only thought that dominated my brain was, *Run.*

Barbara and her attorneys were seated near the windows, to the side of the judge's desk. Doug and I and our representatives sat directly in front of the judge in a row. I would have to lean forward slightly to see Barbara.

The distinguished looking judge posed an impressive picture sitting behind his uncluttered oak desk. His hair was chestnut colored with traces of gray, and he appeared to be in great physical shape beneath his black suit and tightly knotted striped necktie. His all-seeing eyes scrutinized the occupants of the room, almost as if he were contemplating the outcome. He explained that we were here for arbitration and that the decision made today would be binding for all parties concerned.

I stole a glance at the widow by shifting my eyes to the left and leaning forward. She actually didn't have as much to lose as me and Doug. Barbara still had the house, bank accounts, and the condo in Mexico. By comparison, Doug and I had to borrow money against our houses to stay afloat during this time. Both our businesses were hurting because of the time consumed defending and establishing the validity of Father's will. And it was hard to ignore the lawyers' fees that were ticking away like a taxi meter. If we lost, we'd be in debt for God only knows how long.

I abruptly straightened in my chair, startled when I heard Judge Brent ask, "Ms. Hartley, you are the biological daughter of Donald Hartley?"

"Uh. Yes."

The judge asked Father's wife, Doug, and me a few questions to verify some facts. He stated in an unyielding tone, "It is my understanding we're here today regarding a dispute over Mr. Hartley's will."

Barbara blurted out, "There's nothing to dispute! I have a partnership interest in my husband's business. That's how he wanted it and that's how it is." Her head moved up and down as she spoke.

The judge cleared his throat, raised his right hand in the direction of the outburst, and then shifted his eyes and questioned my attorney regarding the allegations just stated.

"We will prove that we are acting in accordance with Mr. Hartley's wishes as outlined in his will and that his children are the only owners of the aforementioned business," she declared.

Barbara shot forward in her chair. "No. No. I am a partner and I can prove it. They're entitled to only half of the business."

I laced my fingers together and re-crossed my legs, trying to resist the urge to scream at her. On the day of the funeral, Barbara had insisted that Doug and I had received nothing. Oh, right—Mariah was entitled to the register book from her grandfather's funeral, which she did receive. Now, today, we were entitled to half the business in her opinion, even though the will stated we received the entire business. The battle lines were drawn. All right, we had moved forward in the last seven months, but it wasn't without an emotional, financial, spiritual, and mental price.

I noticed her hotshot lawyer from the other day was not advising her. The senior partner was frantically whispering in her ear, making a noble attempt to rein her in.

"Please quiet down," the judge ordered. "There will be no talking unless I ask for an answer to a question I pose. Now, Mrs. Hartley, I'd like you to clarify for me what procedures are necessary to run your business."

"Well, you…you get the contract signed, install the sound system for the music to play, the background music, and then there's the tower." She jabbed her thumb westward. "The customers receive monthly billing, which we send out at the end of the month. I know the business inside and out."

I tuned her out as she continued to babble on. The only vibration I could focus on was Doug's thoughts, as I sensed what was mulling around in his mind. *Ask me, judge. Ask me. Please let me answer.*

"Mr. Hartley, I understand you worked with your father frequently in his business, and you are the executor of his will and currently managing the company. What can you tell me about the business?"

Barbara attempted to say something, but the judge swept his hand upward as if waving her away and continued looking at my brother. I could almost feel her coming out of her seat, but she retreated and settled back down.

Doug cleared his throat nervously, uncrossed his legs, and shifted forward in his seat. "We, uh, employ a staff of installers to connect the necessary equipment to get the music up and running." He cleared his throat again and seemed to enter full business mode. "The company employs a sales representative and an office manager. It is vital to the business to keep our sales rep out in the field to generate new business and keep the flow of new contracts coming in." Gathering speed, he continued, "As soon as we are in negotiations, the installers go to the site, estimate the wiring and how long it will take to install the new system. Once that's done, we plan our budget, with our profit added into the installment of the system. We do extensive business with casinos, restaurants, office buildings, and ski areas, providing their background music. The business territory is Reno, Sparks, and Lake Tahoe. The company does experience certain seasonal difficulties with power failures, especially in the wintertime, and when that happens, we are required to get the customers back on-line. We lose about twenty percent of income in the summer because the ski areas are closed."

Interrupting Doug, Father's widow sputtered, "I knew that! He doesn't need to hear all those details."

The judge raised his palm in the air, giving her a stern look, and she quieted down. "I think I have clarification of who is qualified to oversee the business."

She spoke up again. "Judge...I have something to say and I intend to..."

"Wait, Mrs. Hartley," he said sternly, removing his glasses. "It's clear this is not working. I'm going to request we break the sessions up into private conferences with each of the dissenting parties." He signaled to the bodybuilder-type bailiff with massive biceps. "Please have Mr. and Ms. Hartley and their attorneys wait in the conference room until I call for them."

Three long torturous hours of waiting and not knowing, wondering what was going on in the judge's chambers. Confined in the small, colorless conference room, I found myself pacing most of the time. Watching the snow lightly blow outside on this ominous January day was my form of entertainment; or was it a sign of things to come?

Finally, the waiting was over and the muscular bailiff escorted our band of four to the chambers. The judge seemed very attentive as he reviewed the will with us. He questioned Doug extensively about the business. During the full hour of questions, I again became aware of how much my brother was like our father; the tone of his voice and even how he phrased his answers were similar.

The timbre of the judge's voice caught me off guard. "Ms. Hartley. What is the nature of your work?"

"I have my own business. I'm a professional speaker. I support myself and my daughter."

The judge stated, "I take it you're a single parent."

I nodded.

He removed his glasses, placed his hand on one temple, and quietly contemplated. When he finally spoke, he said, "Let me understand this. Mr. Hartley, you have your own business in San Francisco and commute to Reno to manage your father's business as well, and you're a newlywed. And Ms. Hartley, you're also operating your own business, helping your brother with your father's estate, and you are raising a daughter on your own. Am I correct?"

Consecutively, Doug and I replied, "Yes, your Honor."

He considered our answers. "From what I understand, you both have full lives. I must tell you the other side will not give up the business. If we cannot reach an agreement today and the contesting of the will continues, the estate will be depleted. There will be no money left for anyone."

Doug and I sat speechless.

Doug's attorney, who had been quiet up to this time, stated, "Your Honor, I have an idea. Let me see if this might be workable. I would like a few moments to run the numbers on the business and the Nevada house Mrs. Hartley presently owns and is living in."

The judge consented.

Matthew turned to Doug, asking, "Do you have an appraisal on the condo in Mexico?"

"No, not yet."

The next twenty minutes were agonizing, like waiting for a stay of execution. The judge said nothing and was engrossed in reading papers on his desk. Matthew was the only one to speak, asking my brother a couple of questions, but most of time the room was silent. I stopped wringing the damp tissue in my hands when Matthew glanced up from his computer and said, "This is rough, but it gives us a good idea. As things stand today, if Doug and Donna sold off the business, they would have to pay taxes, which would be around $160,000. Mrs. Hartley would still most likely continue to drag out the business ownership battle." He glanced at Doug with a serious expression on his face. "The legal fees would build up and you two would come out with even less. If you did offer Mrs. Hartley half the business, you will be liable for half the taxes and she would be liable for the remaining half."

With a steeled expression on his face, the judge said, "Wait, let me understand this." The room remained noiseless for a few minutes. "What if I put the Nevada residence, the condo in Mexico, and the business into the hat and everything gets sold and the money is divided; half to Mrs. Hartley and the other half divided between Mr. Hartley and Ms. Hartley?"

Doug understood the concept right away. "Show me the numbers," he said to his attorney with energy.

While more numbers were being run, I began to comprehend how important it was to have a business tax lawyer on our team. He could save the day by coming up with a viable plan. My attorney had handled the probate dispute, but this was another matter involving the cash flow, expenses, and tax liabilities. Gazing out the window, I could see darkness approaching. We had been at the courthouse all day.

Doug, the attorneys, and I went into a huddle to discuss the financial outcome. I glanced at the judge once, but he was perusing some papers. Janet scrutinized the numbers, asking questions about real estate commissions, taxes, property values, and all sorts of details I would never have thought of. Information was flying back and forth so quickly that I had difficulty understanding all the facts. Matthew spoke to the judge, relating the details and estimated financial values of the properties and business, plus the tax liabilities. The judge wrote down the information and asked for more details. We spent another hour calculating the final numbers so a decision could be reached.

"I believe we have a workable plan, Donna, and I recommend you accept this proposal," said Janet. "I know you and your brother will lose money, but this would be settled and you could get on with your lives. If you stay in a battle with your stepmother, it could drag on for a long time and there might be very little left. It sounds like her fulltime job is making sure she receives a percentage of the business."

With glossed-over eyes and a shake of my head, I leaned back against my chair. Easy for her to say since she wasn't giving away any of her money. We were giving away our inheritance. The negotiations were beyond my understanding since there were so many variables yet to be determined, like when the business would sell, the value of my father's house in Nevada overlooking Lake Tahoe, and whether the widow would even consider relinquishing the home. "Answer this," I said directly to Janet. "Why did my father write the will one way and now we've turned around and created something else?" Then I stared directly at the judge, who was listening to what I had just said.

Judge Brent removed his glasses before he spoke to me. "Ms. Hartley, I understand your thinking about your father's will. We're in deadlock. It's not uncommon for this to happen. In your case, the other side will not settle unless they get a part of the business." Judge Brent continued, "I have a question for Mr. Hartley."

Doug looked at him intently. "Yes, your Honor?"

"Settling this way, you can stay in control of the business, but how quickly could you sell it? If it isn't sold within, say, three or four months, the ownership is still going to be an issue. Mrs. Hartley will continue to battle for partnership and the right to run the business. I believe her attorneys would accept a reprieve of a few months, but that is all."

My brother pursed his lips in thought, then said, "Since I have been mulling over selling the business, I believe I will have a buyer soon."

"How soon?"

"Maximum, ninety days."

The judge nodded his approval then studied a document he held in front of him. After a minute or so, he placed it back down on his desk and said, "Mr. Hartley, Ms. Hartley, though it is not what your father's will specifies, would you consider dividing the assets in a binding agreement? If both parties are in agreement, I will make it mandatory that the business and Mrs. Hartley's personal residence go up for sale immediately. The Mexico property must also be sold. Proceeds from the sale of all the properties will be divided, half to his widow and a quarter to each of you."

My stomach gnawed with edginess, and I placed my hand on it to silence the grumbling, but I knew my answer. This was an acceptable agreement—not the best, but workable. I looked at my brother. "If this works for you, Doug, okay."

He nodded in agreement. His body slumped over in sheer exhaustion.

"I'm going to ask you folks to return to the conference room for a short wait while I discuss this with the other party, and if we reach an agreement, then bring in the court reporter and finalize the details." The judge excused us.

The wait in the conference room felt like forever. Would my stepmother accept this proposal? The only thing I knew for certain was that she had to have half the business. Living in Tahoe without her husband, the winters would be challenging. She probably wanted to move to a warmer climate so she would sell her house. Outside, headlights streaked along the darkened streets. It had been one nerve-racking day. *Enough already!*

Calling home, I checked on Mariah. "Mommy, when are you coming? Sheba and I miss you."

My heart melted. "I miss you bunches, Little Miss Tulip. I will be on my way soon, but please have Sara give you a bath and read you a few stories before going to sleep."

"I want you to read to me."

In an attempt to change my daughter's mind, I interjected, "I have a great idea. Sara gave you a few books from New Zealand, so have her read those stories. I bet there are some interesting adventures in there."

"Yeah! Thanks, Mommy, I will. Come home soon." Her voice was cheerful.

Whispering into the phone after she hung up, I said, "I hope I will be there soon."

When the door whipped open, we all glanced up, expecting our pleasant but firm bailiff. Instead, it was the widow's attorney, who arrogantly sauntered in as if "Hail to the Chief" were playing in the background.

"Since I am representing Mrs. Hartley, and the judge has presented the final terms, which we have reluctantly agreed to, there is one more issue we need to discuss," he stated in a conceited tone. "My client understands the beachfront condominium in Mexico must be sold." He stuck his hands in his pants pockets and jangled his change while we waited to hear more.

I was hoping we had seen and heard the last of this self-important twit, but such was not the case. Overwrought by what I sensed was another bombshell soon to be dropped, anxiety clenched my stomach, but I managed to keep my mouth shut.

"Since dual ownership of the Mexican condo is out of the question, we recommend you make an offer to buy out Mrs. Hartley's half-share immediately."

As my brother rose from his chair, a nosebleed started. He grabbed a handkerchief from his pocket. "Excuse us. We'd like to discuss this alone, privately, with our lawyers."

"Are you okay?" I ask.

My brother tilted his head back and looked at me with a sideways glance. "Must be the stress," he said through the handkerchief, which was slowly turning scarlet, "but I'm okay."

After the conference door had closed, Doug turned to me and said,

"Donna, I can't handle any more today. You'll have to take over the negotiations for the condo. I want you to buy it. And it has to be done right now, before they change their mind. Let me make you aware of something important. There's a lien on the condo complex. It has to do with irregularities on the part of the builder. It seems he took the money but never transferred the titles. I'm told it could take years to untangle."

Both attorneys sat close by at the conference table but seemed to understand that this conversation was between my brother and me, so they didn't interrupt us.

"Oh great, that makes the condo sound like something I want to own," I said with an acid tone. "Besides, I don't think I can do this. I don't like her attorney."

"You went up against him once before with the music receiving tower and you defeated him. Don't worry about her attorney. You'll like Mexico, and the location is great, half hour over the border in Baja. They even have a kid pool. You'll want to own it." He adjusted his handkerchief and pressed on the bridge of his nose with his other hand.

"Is it worth it? I mean, will we really use it?"

"It's worth it. Trust me; we'll use it a lot. You negotiate the deal."

"What negotiations? I've never even seen the place. I haven't the slightest idea what we'd be buying, not to mention its worth. Remember, Barbara didn't want Mariah and me to visit. A kid would be noisy and make a mess."

"It doesn't matter that you haven't seen it. Look at it this way. We inherited half of it in the agreement we made today. I have been there many times. It's on the beach with a view of the ocean, two bedrooms, you'll like it. We'll work out the money details as soon as you negotiate the price." He dabbed at his nose again.

Negotiate the price? What price? My brother's voice held an underlying desperation that made it clear it was up to me to diffuse the situation. "Do we even know how much it's worth?" I asked.

"Well, I can give you an idea of what he paid for it. In fact, Father first looked at a tiny condo in Southern California that was $750,000 and it wasn't even on the water. That is when he decided to move south of the border. Let me work out some numbers, since Father had it such a short time and he paid for it outright but never received the clear title."

He wrote down what he thought it was worth. After reading the number, I whistled.

"I'll take a second on my house and write her a check. Besides, his wife never liked Mexico," he said as another nosebleed started. His eyes plead with me over the handkerchief clapped to his nose. "Please, Donna, make it happen. I'm too worn out to handle this right now and need to sit here for a few minutes. I know you can do it."

Right, easier said than done. My brother looked drained—even his suddenly pale skin appeared to lack elasticity. He had been the one to make the major decisions concerning the business, since he understood the workings of it, and that had obviously taken its toll. Not only had our grandfather and grandmother died of heart attacks, but our father had just died of a stroke and our mother was in a full-skilled nursing home paralyzed from a stroke. Obviously, heart disease ran in our family, and the way my brother appeared now, I was starting to fear for his health. It was up to me to handle the condo situation.

I shifted Doug's final number around in my muddled brain and slashed away at it, deducting for all the pain and suffering we had endured. Heaven only knows what a lawyer in Mexico would charge to clear the title, and what about the risk involved? Would we ever be the true owners of the property or would it be tied up in Mexican courts?

Janet cleared her throat and said, "Let's go over the numbers." I glared at her.

Come on, intuition, George, Father, help me out here. An amount popped into my head. It was definitely on the short, very, very short side of half.

"No! I have this one and I am not basing what I will offer on value but on sweat, pain, meltdowns, sleepless nights, and time away from my daughter and mother. My brother and I had to endure insults and endless maneuvers from this probate ordeal."

Janet said nothing, only looked at me with a knowing expression that indicated this was my call.

I turned to my brother. "Doug, you have been the front person in this trial. I'll see what I can do now."

I rose, as did my attorney, and we headed for the door. Janet was at my side. "Okay. Let the show begin," I said, attempting to bolster my fading confidence. I needed strength as we headed back into the lion's den.

Barbara's attorney was walking the hallway outside while Barbara sat on a bench. She croaked out the attorney's name when she caught sight of me. He turned and headed toward me. I didn't give him or Janet the chance to speak a word before I said, "Fifty thousand. We will write you a certified check and close no later than two weeks from today."

"That's unacceptable. It's gone up in value and worth four times that."

Janet stared at me. I'm sure she thought that was a low price but maybe a good starting point to negotiate.

Still fresh in my mind was the image of Doug holding a white handkerchief up to his nose, the war-weary lines etched on his face. How had Father's well-intentioned plans come to this? I felt a rush of anger and every bone in my body tingled. I had to stand up and fight, to rid myself once and for all of the rage that had taken over my life. This fighting over my father's will had become a disease that had infected everything and everyone in my life. My gut was screaming at me to trust my intuition and stick to the number I gave, fifty thousand, no matter what. Then, a thought struck me. As of today, the wife's cash flow would be tied up until the business and her house sold. A woman accustomed to having sizeable amounts of cash available would not fare well without it. I was betting she couldn't wait to get rid of the condo in Mexico for whatever cash she could wring out of it.

I turned to her. "There is a problem with the title. The lien is serious. There is no clear ownership. Whether you like it or not, this is my only offer. Take it or leave it."

She instantly snarled, "How could—?"

Her attorney held up his hand. I had often heard other speakers say, "To have leverage, you can't be emotionally attached to whatever it is you want." For me, that wasn't difficult, since I had never seen the condo. What did the building look like? Did the living room or the bedrooms face the ocean? All I knew was that it was in some place on the coast of Mexico called Rosarito Beach. What was Rosarito Beach like anyway? Before Janet could say anything, I nodded at her that we were leaving and we started walking. As I neared the corner, I heard, "Stop!"

I slowly swiveled, standing my ground, scowling at this self-important attorney who had given me dozens of sleepless nights, headaches, and immeasurable anguish

The attorney puffed out his chest and said condescendingly, "My client insists your price is deplorable, but the significance of the lien on the property necessitates that she accept your lowball offer."

Barbara hissed some words to him as her body stiffened with loathing. I heard him murmur, "Take my advice. It will cost them a ton of money to get that lien off the condo, if ever. This is Mexico we're talking about."

I nodded, with a stony face. "I will have the papers drawn up and, after it's signed, messenger you a certified check." Oh no, I was sounding like an attorney.

We turned and walked away. Looking at Janet, almost like what happened wasn't real, I said, "You heard the deal. You get to write it up with all the legal terms."

My attorney smiled with satisfaction.

Don't let life happen to you
Make your life happen

I entered the conference room, glanced at Doug seated next to his attorney, and blurted out, "It's ours. Now you can figure out how to borrow the money. We owe the sum total of fifty thousand."

His eyes widened. "Fifty thousand! How did you negotiate it so cheap?"

"Don't ask me. I don't know if it's a good deal or not. Speaking of which, I sure hope I like Mexico."

By the time I drove back up the mountain from Reno and hugged my front door, it was late, past 9 PM. Mariah was already in bed, and Sara was cleaning up in the kitchen.

"Sorry," I said, throwing my purse and jacket over the back of a chair, "long day. Thanks for staying late."

"Not a problem," she said cheerfully, "see you tomorrow."

Isolating my real emotions behind a front of composure for the entire day had worn me down to the nub. Exhaustion crept through my bones. The big battle was over. Not what I would exactly call a win, but more like a truce.

I peeked in on my daughter sleeping peacefully. Then, I cuddled beside her on the bed and showered her with good-night kisses. She murmured sleepily, "Hi, Mommy."

"Hi, beautiful. I missed you. I am going to sleep here for a while. Mommy is truly tired. Love you."

A tiny voice said, "Love you."

There was a gentle thud on the bed. "Oh, Sheba. You can snuggle too." The only sound I heard was purring.

Lesson Learned:

For the highest good

Chapter Seventeen

The Judgment

In mid-February my brother and I headed in his car to Rosarito Beach, Baja, Mexico, located thirty minutes south of the California border. Compared to the Hawaii I knew so well, Mexico seemed more arid with a choppy infrastructure. Houses and commercial buildings along the highway were unfinished and abandoned. A pungent odor penetrated the air. At least I didn't see shacks lining the side of the road in Rosarito Beach, as they did on the hillsides of Tijuana. No doubt for me, this was culture shock.

Doug and I had decided this was to be a working trip to see the condo, have the title of ownership deeded to us, and transfer all the utilities to our names. Though I had initially wanted to bring Mariah along, I decided she would demand too much attention, and, of course, would want to spend playtime on the beach, so I had her stay home with Sara. It was always difficult for me to leave her behind, and my heart ached to be with her. My next trip to Mexico would be with my daughter. Doug's wife, Aunt Donna, had to teach at her middle school in San Francisco, so the trip was to be a siblings-only affair.

My brother turned into the gated complex and handed the guard the paperwork allowing us to enter. Was I expecting more greenery, lush flowers, like in Hawaii? They were definitely lacking as I took in the stark pinkish tan building before me. When we reached our unit on the second floor, Doug set down his briefcase and unlocked the door. He hesitated and glanced at me, then let it swing open.

Walking into the condo, my eyes welled up and I swallowed hard to keep tears from streaming down my cheeks. "Everything is gone!" I stood in the center of the room, slowly rotating and taking it all in. "What are those wires?"

Sympathetically, Doug informed me, "A chandelier hung over the dining room table."

"Chandelier! Where is it?" I gasped. "The dining room table?" Clutching my hands together. "What are all those holes in the wall?"

"A large mirror hung there."

"How could she do this?"

"Take it easy," Doug said brusquely. "Everything is fixable or replaceable. We'll drive over the border and buy new kitchen stuff and furniture. We'll fill the car with the small items and bring them back. The large furniture can be delivered."

Tears dribbled down my cheeks as I ambled listlessly into the kitchen, yanking open drawers and cabinet doors. Stripped and barren, nothing, not so much as a plastic fork hidden in the cracker crumbs was in the room. Pausing as a sudden wave of sadness swept over me. Before purchasing the property, Father had never spent much time in a tropical climate, so Mexico had held appeal for him. I remembered him telling me how relaxed he felt in his reclining chair, gazing out at the water. He had mentioned the pool and the palm trees blowing in the breeze again and again. And now it was reduced to this.

"I can't believe it," I said. "She came down here and took everything. She stripped this place clean. I was fooled into believing we had a binding agreement. She stole everything!" I shouted. "It would cost too much to go back to court and fight her. She won again! We...we can't afford to fix up this place."

Softly, with admiration in his voice, my brother said, "You made that possible."

"What are you talking about?"

"I am the executor of his will and we received clearance to use the bank account I opened after Father's death. You sold his car and that money is in the account. We have enough to remodel and have the lien taken off the property."

"We do? We can remodel and everything?"

"We'll make it work."

I glanced around the open space again, my heart beginning to lift with possibilities swirling in my head. "You know, it's probably better I never visited the condo with Mariah. The stepmother insisted Father needed his rest when he came down here. If I'd have seen the condo before, I would have something to compare all this loss to. I would be screaming mad instead of just being angry. Well, at least you were here many times..." I trailed off, my bitterness too much for even me to handle.

Doug recognized he should change the subject. "Wait," he said, "here is the best part." He pulled on the floor-to-ceiling window coverings and slowly revealed the view of the ocean.

"Wow! It's magnificent," I said in awe of the splendid view.

The panorama of the Pacific Ocean beyond the sliding glass doors was more than I had imagined. An ideal picture of peace, the shimmering blue water washed onto the pristine beach, where pale grey seagulls convened to peck and bob in the shallows, scavenging for food. The sky was splashed with puffy white clouds and a brilliant sun headed toward the horizon. I could have been contemplating a similar view during cocktail hour at an elegant resort anywhere in the world. Memories of a rosy pink Hawaiian sunset stirred deep in my mind as I recalled my most serene and introspective hours spent looking out over the ocean. Thirty years ago, I made a promise to myself that I would someday own a condo overlooking the Pacific Ocean. At the time, I was envisioning the place to be in Hawaii, not Baja. *Next time I visualize a dream, I have to be more specific with the details.*

Doug opened the slider as I inhaled the fresh air. "I love it; the view, the sound of the ocean." I chuckled. "I always wanted a condo on the water."

Opening his briefcase, Doug lifted out a half-dozen legal pads and a couple of pens. "We should get started," he stated as he handed me a pad and pen. "I'll make a list of repairs and you pick a room and start making a list of what we need."

"List! We need everything."

"Just in case, I threw two sleeping bags and some pillows into my car. We'll need them for later," he said.

He knew. He expected Barbara to pull something like this, but I wondered if he thought it would be this bad. Well, at least the refrigerator and stove were still in place.

Sitting down on the floor, I started a kitchen list: paper towels, cutlery, dishes, glassware, coffee cups, pots, frying pan, cutting board, and continued for three pages.

Then I moved to the first bedroom and tackled another list. Doug strolled around inspecting the holes in the walls and missing light bulbs from the track lighting, all the time adding to his growing inventory.

He noticed I was sitting in the middle of the empty bedroom with only sunlight from the windows and my list for company. "Why don't you go downstairs and check out the pool area? There's a communal baby pool and a Jacuzzi too. It's on the first floor. Walk toward the ocean. You can't miss it." He turned and left without waiting for my reply.

It took a few minutes to grasp what he had said because I was so immersed in my list. Slowly rising, I glanced around the condo. *This could have been so much easier. Civil. It didn't have to be like this.*

Strolling out of the building, I found myself murmuring while approaching the pool, "Oh, this is breathtaking." Sliding into a lounge chair, I inhaled the fresh salt air and relished the approaching sunset. A few palm trees swayed in the breeze as I gazed at the rolling waves on the horizon.

A couple of diehard kids were still playing in the children's pool, but the large adult pool was empty. Watching the children frolic and splash, Mariah came to mind. I wished she had been able to spend time here with her Poppy. Memories, I wanted to create memories with her, because sometimes that is all you have.

Closing my eyes, I felt the warmth of the last remaining sunrays on my body.

I am sorry. Forgive me. I know you and Mariah will love Mexico as much as I did.

My eyes popped open. "Father, is that you? Are you here?" I sat there waiting to hear more. Nothing. Nada, only the sound of crashing waves on the beach in the distance. Was my fatigue running away with me, or maybe not?

Lesson Learned:

Believe in your dreams

Chapter Eighteen
Sign the Papers

Within sixty days, my brother had two potential buyers for my father's business. I wasn't exactly sure how he did it. All I knew was that I was gathering information and forwarding comparisons and facts every few days. Even more astonishing, each successive potential buyer had outbid the previous offer. Perhaps this entire tribulation had taken a turn for the better. Could the days 'til the final settlement be numbered?

The amazing fact was that all the bids were over the appraised value of the business. I could only wish the extra money Doug and I would gain would pay our attorney fees and leave some left over, but a part of me was still afraid to anticipate that could happen.

Yes, I wanted to jump up and down when the final offer was accepted by Doug, our attorneys, and me. Our stepmother's lawyer was then notified that the offer was legitimate and had actually exceeded the appraisal. The documents had to be signed by all parties and returned to the buyer within forty-eight hours. Doug and I signed immediately and sent the documents back. The last signature would soon be delivered to the buyer. A treat was in order, and Mariah and I indulged ourselves at the ice cream shop.

When forty-eight hours had passed, Doug phoned. Before he could say anything, I chimed in, "You did a great job."

"His wife," Doug said in a disgusted tone, "didn't sign the papers. She didn't accept the offer. She has to sign to make this a valid sale."

His news sent a blitz of possibilities spinning through my head, each worse than the last. Finally I croaked out, "You signed, I signed, and she has to sign!"

"We missed the forty-eight hour window."

"What do you mean?" I demanded.

"Once the sale offer is agreed upon, the papers are sent out for all signatures, and the money is held in escrow. Matthew cleared it and Janet cleared it and even their attorney verbally approved the offer, but she didn't sign the papers. The deal is off."

We both let that sink in for a moment.

"The buyer was livid," Doug said tightly. "Screamed at me because he borrowed the money and now that the deal has gone sour, he wants to sue me for the interest he owes the lender." He released a huge sigh of frustration. "He's threatening to sue for thousands of dollars."

"I'm calling my attorney to see what she can do."

After answering the phone, Janet exclaimed, venting her annoyance, "I cannot believe the woman did not sign. Doesn't she realize this is a viable offer that exceeded the appraisal and is sanctioned by a court order she signed to sell the business?"

For the next thirty days, the waiting game was pure hell. I attempted to work, but my mind was wracked with worry on how to pay my attorney, feed my daughter, and visit my mother. I took a line of credit out on my house to keep up with the bills. Doug was overwhelmed, pursuing an ongoing communication with the former buyer, who had since put his initial anger on hold thanks to Doug's lawyer and my brother's constant phone calls.

Many times during those thirty days, I asked myself what were my stepmother's motives for not signing. I could only guess that on some level, she believed she was entitled to the entire business. It didn't make sense, it wasn't rational, and once again we were forced to pay the price.

As fate would have it, the buyer still wanted the company and made a second offer for the business. Doug and I signed the new documents and returned them immediately. Again, there was only one signature missing. I prayed every night that somehow the stepmother's attorney would show her the benefit of signing this set of documents by instilling in her the threat that if she didn't, we would all have to go back to court.

The next evening, after we signed the papers right before dinner, the phone rang. I was sure it was my brother, who had called throughout the day to see if I had heard from my attorney and whether the widow had signed the papers. We understood that we were at the end of the ninety-day extension the judge had granted us to sell the company.

"You can celebrate. The ink is dry." I heard papers shuffling in the background as Janet said, "She signed the papers in the eleventh hour. This is how it works. It will take at least thirty days to close escrow and deal with other pending probate matters before the proceeds are divided between the three of you. I will coordinate all the details with your brother's attorney."

"Okay," was all I could say, too stunned to say anything else.

"If you recall, during the arbitration, I had written into the binding agreement that half the value of Mrs. Hartley's house will be paid to you and Doug from the business escrow. In other words, you two will be paid in advance for the sale of her house. Reason being, she could take years to sell the place, and I didn't feel you should have to wait. If it sells for more than the appraised value, you and Doug will also be entitled to half of whatever that turns out to be. There are still taxes and business expenses to pay out of probate and attorney fees."

"I see," I said. "In the confusion I had forgotten you did that. I am so glad it's over. Wait, it is over, isn't it?" I questioned.

"Yes, it should be over, barring any unforeseen details."

That is where my stepmother is brilliant, creating unforeseen details.

A month later, my brother surprised me with a visit to my house. "Got anything stronger than herbal tea?" he asked, conferring a sly smile while opening a portfolio. "I'm writing you a check. After all we've been through, this calls for a celebration."

"A check?"

"Remember, the cost of the attorneys, the taxes for the business, and the accountant fees are already taken out of this amount," Doug remarked.

Glancing over his shoulder as he wrote, I joked, "Wow, we still have money left over after all the fees and taxes." I smiled a big toothy grin, which seemed like the first time I had smiled in a long time. Joking, I said, "Hope this check doesn't bounce."

"If it does, we'll both go to jail."

So what if it wasn't anywhere near a windfall? I still felt like I had won the lottery. I had hoped so many times, even prayed and asked for help, but in reality I wasn't exactly sure this day would ever come.

Maybe this was about relationships: having an honest relationship with my brother, my attorney, myself, and even my father and Barbara. Not trying to screw over anyone but only wanting what was promised.

Doug laid the check down in front of me and folded his hands. He donned his brotherly demeanor and said, "This will help you. Pay your bills."

Looking at the check and then glancing at him, I almost couldn't believe this was happening. I was speechless.

"Have you given any thought to what you're going to do with your share of the money?"

Turning his question over in my mind, I hesitated, then answered, "Recently, I've been taking inventory of some much overdue home improvements: kitchen floor, carpeting, energy efficient windows to stop the winter draughts from blowing in, and maybe a new fence for the backyard." I continued, "Also, my car is going on eleven years with high mileage. And a new SUV is in my future, with no car payments." I kept staring at the check, shaking my head.

Doug said, "Sounds good. It's worth it to invest in your house."

"First thing I'll do is pay off my line of credit that I borrowed to live on during this journey." I laughed. "Journey, what a nice word to describe this nightmare, since I used four-letter words when I was living it." I chuckled.

Doug agreed. "Here, let me outline the other details." He showed me how he planned the budget on his ledger and allocated the amount to be paid back on the line of credit he used from his house to pay Barbara off. "Let's do the math regarding what we want to set aside to finalize the condo's ownership and keep ahead of the dues and normal maintenance."

"Are you sure we're going to own the condo? I mean, get the lien off our condo from the builder? I know it's complicated. The builder wouldn't accept our offer on the first attempt, so how much extra money are we going to have to pay in Mexico to gain true ownership?"

"Don't know yet. We'll keep working at it. In the meanwhile, you open the bank account in both our names and I'll transfer the money in."

"Fine, but soon as I can catch up here, I'm going back to Pennsylvania to see Mom; John needs a break. He's there every night making sure she falls asleep. It's been years now that she's been in the nursing home." Glancing at my brother as he stretched out his feet, leaned back, and listened intensely. I continued, "I'll take Mariah and spend two weeks." For a moment I was lost in contemplation. "For stepparents, there is a world of difference. Our stepmother wanted all the money and quickly pulled the plug on Father, whereas John is selling everything they own to make sure that Mother is taken care of."

"I know." Doug shifted forward and pushed the check closer in my direction. "Things should go smoother now."

"I certainly hope so." But that gnawing feeling was back in my gut. What was my intuition signaling to me now?

Lesson Learned:

Honest relationships are essential

Chapter Nineteen

The Warriors Win

"What do you mean we are going back to court?" I screamed into the phone. "We can't. We had binding arbitration!" It was late January, almost a year since the court ruling with Barbara.

"Donna, calm down!" Doug said. "I spoke with my attorney and Barbara wrote the judge informing him she has an offer on the house that is for more than the appraisal and we are not entitled to the extra amount. She stated that she never agreed to it."

"This is insane! We all signed the binding arbitration. You sold the business for more than the appraised value and she received her extra share." My blood boiled. "We have court-approved arbitration papers stating that if we gave up half the business, even though the will wasn't written that way, every party would accept the binding arbitration. The word is binding."

Doug attempted to speak, but I interrupted. "Three months prior, do you recall that incident? We paid our share of the business taxes to the Internal Revenue Service, okay, all fine and good. Oh, and the widow refused to pay her half. She did a complete about-face, saying we owned the business and were liable for all the taxes. She insisted we gave her part of the business out of the goodness of our hearts." My voice raised a notch. "After weeks of pushing paper back and forth to the IRS to prove she owned half the business, and was liable for her share of the taxes, they finally agreed to take the matter under review. It was settled in our favor, but how many thousands did that cost us? Five thousand dollars! And now this! Attorney fees. Time. More money…" Coughing, I couldn't complete the sentence.

"Are you all right?"

"No! I'm crazy. This is making me ill. I can't handle much more."

The following week was occupied with phone calls to Janet asking for her advice and ranting that I didn't want to go back to court again. Janet insisted all four of us had to meet to discuss the upcoming court appearance.

Ten days later, here Doug and I were with our lawyers at yet another strategy meeting at my lawyer's office.

"I can tell you this," Janet said, "the judge is not happy with Mrs. Hartley writing directly to him rather than going through her attorney. It's not legally advisable. But it's also my understanding she currently does not have an attorney representing her."

I quickly asked, "Why not?"

"She fired both of them."

I actually chuckled. "Hope they were paid up front or they're going to have to fight for their fees."

"You called it. There is a lien on the house for her attorney fees."

I shot my brother a quick glance. Doug gave a nod, just like he did when he was a kid, and we understood each other without saying a word.

"I've seen this scenario play out in court before. The judge will ask where her attorney is and then he'll spend the court's precious time questioning her. Since arbitration is final and binding, and there is a lien on the house representing both of you, in the event it is sold for more than the appraisal, she'll be required to settle with you two. We're predicting the judge will not modify the arbitration agreement, and your father's wife will have to pay both of you what you're entitled to."

On a gloomy, cold day two days later, we once again entered the brittle silence of a Reno courtroom. A massive bailiff with a gold crown glittering on his front tooth smiled broadly as he stood to the right of the judge's bench. I couldn't say what it was, but something about him had a calming effect on my jangled nerves. If I had been watching this scene play out on television, I would consider it a soap opera. Or maybe a sitcom. The only difference was that it was real life...it was my life.

Judge Brent entered the courtroom in his robe, casting a cursory glance around the room. His eyes settled on our stepmother, and he asked, "Mrs. Hartley, who is representing you? You may be represented by an attorney or yourself. If you have no attorney, the court can appoint one for you."

"I am," Barbara stated just above a whisper. She appeared nervous as she fiddled with her blouse.

A rustle of paper and a long pause later, the impressive judge seated at his bench said with a serious, no-nonsense attitude, "Mrs. Hartley, since you petitioned the court to hear this matter, let's begin with you."

Doug glanced my way, saying softly, "Judge Brent doesn't look too happy to see us again."

I gave my brother a quick nod and confirmed, "I see that too." The judge had settled this case before, and now here he was wasting his time ruling again.

One after another, the questions rolled off the judge's tongue. He continually removed his glasses, saying, "Let me clarify what you're telling me, Mrs. Hartley. And remember, I was the sitting judge for the binding arbitration. I know exactly how I ruled. All parties agreed to and are bound by the final arbitration. Do you understand that, Mrs. Hartley?"

Red-faced, she said, "But, I didn't know I would have to pay his children extra money if the house sold for more than the appraised value. That should be my money. My attorney didn't tell me. That's why I fired him."

The judge spent two hours questioning our stepmother. Refreshing her memory by reading the pertinent text from the arbitration agreement, the judge emphasized, "If you have a problem with your attorney, you can take it up with him or file a complaint independent of what is happening here today. This arbitration is binding. I will hear no further arguments."

At that moment, I squeezed my eyes tightly shut and prayed that never again would I undergo this sort of ordeal. I used to be fearless and passionate about my life, but this drawn-out battle had me complaining and fighting depression. What had George said about staying away from negative people? "Their downbeat vibration will fester in you, causing you to doubt yourself or even create a sickness."

When I opened my eyes, my gaze was drawn upward to the left corner of the courtroom, where I sensed my father. *Are you here? Tell me this is done. Did it take this trial for you and me to understand each other? We do have similar traits. Yes, I am stubborn and determined like you. It was difficult for me to forgive. I must...I must, for my daughter's sake. The negative patterns of my family have to be changed. I want to be a better parent.* My thought process stopped. There was something else in there, but it wouldn't surface. Again my thoughts flooded my mind. *I hope, no, I truly pray, Father, that you and I have healed. Sorry we didn't heal when you were alive. Sorry we had to wait 'til after your death. Because our relationship was not based on trust and communication, I have been afraid my entire life to allow a caring man into my world. I must heal and let go of the past, creating space for my future to manifest.*

An instant later, my attorney's voice yanked me back to reality. "Your Honor, I have prepared documents stating when the Nevada property, Mrs. Hartley's residence, sells, we will settle the lien, and the forthcoming money will be divided immediately."

"Have the documents delivered to my chambers this afternoon and I will sign them," the judge said with finality to his voice.

Doug's attorney spoke next. "Also, in light of your ruling, I would like the funds that were held back from the business for tax purposes to be released, since Mr. Hartley is executor and their side has paid their share."

"Deliver the documents, I'll sign them," Judge Brent answered.

Just like that, the hearing was over, and next we were all standing as the judge exited the courtroom. *That's it,* I thought, *two and a half years of my life wrapped up in mere seconds.*

Turning to Janet, I asked, "Is it over? Is there anything else that can go wrong?"

Janet smiled, her blonde hair gleaming like a halo above her head even in the dim courtroom lights. "It's over. When you've been on the treadmill this long, it's hard to believe that you can finally get off."

"Doug," I said, "the system works. We did it."

He gave me a wary look. "The shootout's over, but the other side hasn't surrendered yet. She hasn't sold the house, and we still don't have a clear condo title in our names. The Mexico system has to be dealt with."

An unexpected surge of nausea welled up in me. "I'm not feeling well. Excuse me." I rushed to the ladies room and took refuge at a white porcelain sink as a sudden onset of chills and dizziness overcame me. I clutched the edge of the sink. Staring at my pale reflection, I jerked back. My face appeared strange, worn—no, different. There was a depth of knowing in it that I hadn't seen before. I was suddenly aware of the anxiety and fear I had stuffed down for over two years. It had been all-consuming. As George would say, "There is a spiritual lesson from everything that crosses your path. You can't say something is right or wrong. The message always is: What is the lesson?"

Heal now
Heal later
Heal at death
Heal after death
You must heal

I heard the bathroom door open, and Janet stepped inside. Fine lines of concern were etched across her forehead. "Are you okay?"

"Yes." I pulled down several paper towels, ran them under cold water, and began dabbing them on my face. "Thanks. You were a guiding force though this unbelievable ordeal."

Janet smiled and touched my arm. "You're welcome," she said.

I adjusted my black knit dress, thinking, *I'm tired of wearing these dismal, dark colors. Please let this period of my life be over.* As the thought crossed my mind, a piercing sensation shot through my heart. Attempting to ignore the feeling, I tossed the saturated paper towels in the trash and picked up my purse, preparing to leave. I couldn't shake the inner knowing that, even after the judge's ruling, something was plaguing me, like the rug was going to be pulled out from under me.

In the car, with only the hum of the engine to keep me company, my thoughts drifted to my sage mentor. We'd had hundreds of conversations over the years, and George never faltered in his belief that taking the high road was the only path. That above all the muck and mire on this planet there was a higher purpose and that all of us were accountable to a higher spiritual karma. Completing this trial was a spiritual victory for me. I was rewarded monetarily, but the most important outcome was that I understood my father more and had the opportunity to heal with him. I never thought our healing would come as a result of a drawn-out probate trial. My mentor was right when he said, "Man's maneuvers are trumped by spiritual enlightenment."

Turning down the street to my house, the stately pine trees in my yard shimmered in the car's headlights. I grinned.

Lesson Learned:
Power of spiritual wisdom

Part III

What, More Healing!

Chapter Twenty
March 1st Strikes Again

It was a day of celebration, for it had been exactly twenty-four years since I was in a life-changing plane crash at the Los Angeles International Airport. I always planned an event on March 1st, nothing big, just an acknowledgement of survival. With no champagne or even a handsome guy by my side, this year I decided cross country skiing would be ideal, with the snow glittering and the sun shining though the pine trees. I yearned to spend time in the serenity of the woods, gliding along the white crystal, appreciating the wisdom I had gleaned from the crash. *Without a doubt, there is a higher purpose to life, even with all the madness that happens.*

It had been a year since my brother and I had last been in court battling our stepmother, and now there was time for my spiritual quest. Meditating, writing in my journal, exercising, cross country and downhill skiing, but I was tired most of the time, I chalked it up to stress. The clear title to the condo in Mexico had yet to be obtained in spite of a half dozen trips to Baja, and our stepmother's house had not sold. I had visited my mother three times in the past year, and Mariah was able to come with me. My daughter talked nonstop to Nana about books, travel, cartoons, clothes, her friends, school, the cat, her fish, and whatever else popped into her mind. I don't believe my mother understood half of it, but it seemed to keep her alert.

Mom's condition had not changed. Still in the full-skilled nursing home, she was fed mashed foods at every meal and lifted in and out of her bed by a mechanical hoist. She had increased her ability to speak a few more words, which were choppy and throaty, but I managed to understand most of what she was saying.

One day, as I sat at her bedside, I could see she was struggling to say something. "What is it, Mother?" I asked gently.

"I need you....help... me," Mother said, taking in a few gulps of air.

Moving my wooden chair closer to her bed, I replied, "Sure, Mom, can I get you something to drink? Is that what you want?" She gave a whimper, and then her face scrunched up and she began to sob. "Mom, please," I said, grabbing her right hand, which was jerking in the air. "I'm here for you. It's okay. Please relax. I love you." I gently smoothed her hand in mine, rubbing her fingers in an attempt to calm her.

"You need to...you...you...die first. So...I can...die. I...I...I...afraid."

"Mom! Mom, you are fine. That is crazy talk." I shook my head, thinking I must have misunderstood her. She couldn't be asking me to kill myself. The drugs. It must be the drugs.

Her right hand jerked away, grabbing her hair and pulling at it as she mumbled between sobs, "Die...die...first...I can die....then."

Shocked, I sat there staring at the woman I loved, not believing her words. Tearing up and filled with emotion, I slowly said, "I have Mariah to raise. I must stay with her."

"Doug...ra...raise her. He...more...money."

My mouth dropped open. I shook my head. I started to speak but was interrupted by a nurse who had arrived to change my mother's bedding. I quickly moved out of the room, almost sprinting down the hall and out of the building. Running 'til my side ached, gasping for air through my tears, I buckled as my knees collapsed onto the cold, hard ground. "No! No! I can't." Mother's request brought a chill to my heart that I couldn't name and couldn't shake off.

On every visit after that, she begged me to die. I still couldn't believe I was hearing her correctly, but she insisted my brother had more to offer than me so he could raise Mariah and that if I died first she wouldn't be so afraid to follow. To hear her cry was heart-wrenching, and even when I'd leave her at the end of our visits, I could still hear her sobs bellowing from her room as I walked down the hall.

I loved my mother, but these conversations tormented me. I didn't tell anyone about them—not even John. Maybe there was a part of me that didn't want to believe my mother would ask such a thing from me.

As I sought to puzzle out this confusing turn of events, I recalled that George had often insisted that no one was free of karmic lessons— that we were all held accountable for our actions sooner or later. I was realizing that my mother had chosen to put off her lessons 'til the end of her life. I remembered how I argued with George over this topic at several early breakfast chats, adamant that many people cheated and lied yet their lives were better than mine.

"Not true," George said, shaking his head, "everyone someday will be held responsible."

I wondered whether my mother was now facing her past and the demons that had controlled her for so long. It was sad to witness and was a strong reminder for me to learn my lessons when they happened and not to put them off 'til later. Who knows, they might add up karmic interest and be more difficult to deal with later in life. *Looks like you were right again, George*, I thought.

Before his death, George had used dozens of parables, or what I called Georgeisms—well, really I called them blooming Georgeisms—to help me understand the lessons I had to endure.

Life holds for each of us
lessons to understand and work through

March 1st was my opportunity to reflect on what I had accomplished. My mentor was adamant that each lesson must be learned or it would be repeated. Therefore, I was to stay on the path of healing no matter the time or the cost.

Whoever said life was a bowl of round little red things with pits? Yesterday my lovely little white fluff ball, Sheba, came down with an infection. Administering the medicine the vet had prescribed was not the easiest task. That smart little kitty of mine somehow knew when I had the medicine in my hand, and she scooted right under the bed to the very middle where she couldn't be reached.

Now, with skis rattling in the back of the car, a quiet Mariah and I were on the way to her pediatrician. My feverish daughter had woken this morning complaining of a sore throat while tears filled her eyes from the pain. Pushing her finger against the window glass, Mariah said hoarsely, "Mommy, there's the place you found me walking on the side of the road."

"You're right," I said, shivering at the thought of what could have happened during that harrowing experience.

Last week, Mariah had her entire elementary school turned upside down. I told her to take the bus home, but she had forgotten my instructions. As the bus drove away, Mariah sat perched behind a snow bank to wait for me at school. Meanwhile, I was waiting at the bus stop near our home.

The busload of kids had come and gone, but no Mariah. Panic set in. I ran home called the school, but no one had seen her. Then I called her girlfriends' houses, but again no one remembered seeing her. I frantically peered out the window, searching the empty street, trying to decide what to do next. Call the sheriff or get in the car and start looking for her myself? What if she showed up at the house and I wasn't there? A chill snaked up my spine and I knew instantly what I had to do. I needed to mentally contact my daughter. I had told her if anything scary ever happened to use her mind and send me a message. Spinning around my head was the question, *Mariah, where are you? Mariah, tell Mom where you are. Where are you?* It seemed an eternity until I sensed something.

Mommy, school. Come for me. School. Come for me.

Grabbing my purse, I leapt into the car and gunned the engine. Focusing on driving as fast as I could down Highway 28, my peripheral vision caught a flash of pink. Squinting my eyes, I saw more pink. It was Mariah's parka. My six-year-old was walking by herself on the side of the highway, heading toward home. I slammed on the brakes, pulled onto the shoulder, and jumped out of the car.

Mariah cried out, "Mommy, Mommy, you came for me!" Tears shone in her eyes. She gulped in air as she continued, "I kept repeating, 'Mommy, I'm at school. I'm at school. I'm at school. Come for me'."

Wrapping her shivering little body in a huge bear hug, I choked out, "I love you so much. I'm glad you're safe."

"Mommy I love…you," Mariah sniffled.

"Did you forget to take the bus?"

"Ohhhhh. I got mixed up. Ohhhhhh. I forgot. I thought you were picking me up at school. I sat next to the snow pile waiting and, when you didn't come, I thought you were home sick in bed again. I'm sorry," she said, swiping her tears with grubby mittens. "I started walking home to help you. I knew you haven't been feeling good. I thought you were too sick to drive."

"I've been sick a lot lately, but I'm going to get all better soon." I dispensed another squeeze. Everything made sense now. The teachers who were searching for her didn't see her because she was hidden by the high snow bank.

A swell of parental pride surged up. "Mariah, you are a survivor. Being a survivor runs in this family." What had I heard in the plane accident? That I would have a daughter late in life and her destiny was to be a leader. Holding her hand in mine, we walked to the car. "Let's go home. I'll call the school, tell them you're fine, and then make you a snack."

Her hazel eyes focused on me as she softly said, "Yummy!"

It was also the ideal time to review what to do if Mom was late. As a parent, when you think you have all the bases covered, something unexpected keeps you running them again and again.

Back in the present, she was examined by the pediatrician, who confirmed that Mariah had a strep throat. Next stop, the pharmacy. At home, I settled my daughter on the sofa with a blanket beside my other little sick kid, Sheba. So much for my grand plans to celebrate my special survival day with skiing. Well, the thought was there, but my daughters had their own agendas and I felt a little under the weather myself. *Please, not another cold coming on, or even worse, the flu.* A nap would be my celebration this day. Yes, a siesta was in order.

As I sang a lullaby to the girls, they drifted off, closing their eyes. They looked so adorable snuggled up with one another. *Sleepy time for me. A midday nap, how fantastic is this.*

In my bedroom, fluffing my pillow, I felt my body unwind. Turning sideways, a sharp pain flashed through my left thigh. Quickly I touched my throbbing leg where, during a routine visit, the dermatologist had removed a blackish mole two days earlier. I'd been so involved in taking care of my family I hadn't stopped to think about it until now.

March 1st and nothing has happened. A chill penetrated my spine as a clump of snow smacked loudly against my bedroom window, startling me.

Lesson Learned:

Celebrate each day

Chapter Twenty-One

It Can't Be

Drifting off to dreamland, I was startled by a shrill sound. *Drat. Some nap.* Sitting up, I fumbled for the phone. Clearing my throat, I attempted to sound awake. "Hello, this is Donna."

"Doctor Mandell here. Your report came back regarding the skin lesion I removed from your left thigh. I'm afraid the news isn't good."

The serious tone of his voice concerned me. "What do you mean?"

"There is no easy way to say this other than to come out with it. You have melanoma. It's very serious. It's in an advanced stage."

"Melanoma? What...what are you telling me?"

"There are four stages of this type of cancer. I don't mean to scare you, but it's important you understand the seriousness of what I'm saying. You're at an advanced stage. You have a form of cancer that, should it spread to your lymph nodes, can invade your entire body."

My lips were frozen together. Struck dumb, I couldn't speak. *Cancer. It can't be.*

"Did you understand what I said? This is very serious," Doctor Mandell continued in his professional voice.

Tossing back the comforter, I stared at my thigh. "I need to know more."

"Advanced melanoma must be treated immediately. It spreads rapidly and can become life-threatening. At this point we don't know if your cancer has spread. You cannot procrastinate making a decision regarding your treatment. There's no time to waste. Write down this information."

I reached for my bedside pad and pen. *This can't be happening. Oh, Mariah. What about Mariah?*

"You are going to call the University of California San Francisco Melanoma Center and get an appointment ASAP. They specialize in treating this type of cancer. You'll require immediate surgery."

My hand shook uncontrollably. *Surgery.* "Please, repeat who I should call." As he did so, I scrawled the names and numbers like a child, taking up most of the page.

"Write down my home phone. I want you to call me any time," he said.

Another page of quivering scrawl.

"Have you written everything down? It's very important."

"Yes." Trying to decipher my penmanship. "I think I have it all."

"Good. It's Friday, four o'clock. I'm going to call the UC San Francisco Melanoma Center right away, tell them you are my patient, and alert them that you require an appointment immediately. I will forward your medical records to them and also fax you a copy along with the lab report."

I mumbled my fax number.

"Please call the Melanoma Center after we hang up. This is urgent."

"I will. Uh…"

His tone softened. "I want you to know I have never lost a patient who I referred to the Melanoma Center. They will take excellent care of you." Silence. "Are you okay?"

Never lost a patient? "Uh-huh." I was processing what he said. *How could I have cancer? No one in my family had cancer. A mistake. The report must be wrong. It's possible. Isn't it?*

"It worries me that you're so quiet. Do you have someone with you?"

"No. No, I don't. Oh, my daughter, but she's sleeping. She's sick. You sure about this? It's skin cancer? Could there be a mistake?"

"No mistake. I'm going to hang up now. Call UC San Francisco before they close. Call me if you need anything, even this weekend."

The phone fell to the floor as my body crumpled. Crossing my arms tightly, I rocked back and forth. No, this could not be happening to me! No! No! No! My mentor predicted I would have three major life lessons. I always questioned how I would know. His reply was that without a shadow of a doubt I would know.

March 1st fate strikes again. First a plane accident, now melanoma, couldn't be a mistake. It was a message. Tears blurred my vision so badly, I couldn't find the phone for a while.

Muttering into the phone, I punched in the numbers while my hand was shaking. A sweet high-pitched recorded voice announced a menu of selections to choose from. I pushed the number for new patients.

"Please leave your name and number and we'll call you as soon as possible. Before we return your call, you must fax or mail current patient information, lab results, your biopsy report, health insurance information, and your referring doctor's name."

I scribbled to write down the Melanoma Center's fax number the recorded voice gave me with an unsteady hand so I could send my medical information. Dr. Mandell had said he would send the records himself, but I didn't want to take any chances—two sets would be better than none. Attempting to stand, my legs failed me. Trying slowly, with the help of the nightstand, I stood and tore the scrawled numbers I had just written from a notepad. Taking several deep breaths, I managed to shuffle to the living room to check on the girls. Still asleep on the sofa. *I must live to see them both grow up.*

With carefully calibrated steps, I forced myself to place one foot in front of the other as I climbed the stairs to my office, counting the steps... *one...two...three...four...five...six...seven...* Retrieving my medical records that my doctor had immediately sent over from the fax machine, my state was surreal. *This is happening to someone else, not me.*

Doctor Mandell was adamant I required an appointment ASAP. I punched the Melanoma Center's fax number into the machine and sent my medical files and Doctor Mandell's referral letter. I grabbed the phone, connected with the Melanoma Center menu, and left my name and number on the machine. So desperate was I to talk to a human being, the idea of baring my soul and records to a faceless voice without a body freaked me out.

The third time I called, the offices had closed for the weekend. What would I do until Monday? Contemplate my mortality? *What if I di…di…I can't even think the word.*

Lessons Learned:

Face your destiny

Chapter Twenty-Two
Girlfriends to the Rescue

When Joan answered the phone, I sputtered a few garbled words.

"Donna, what is it? What's wrong?" she asked in a worried tone.

"I have ca…cancer. The doctor said its melanoma. It's…my leg, my thigh."

"Oh, oh, I'm very sorry." Joan's voice changed from her normal upbeat tone to one of concern. I heard her inhale a deep breath.

"I go to the dermatologist. I'm careful because of my fair skin," I sniffled.

"I know you are."

"Mariah…Mariah! I can only think of my daughter and what might happen to her. She is so young. She needs a mother."

"Donna. Please try to calm yourself."

"I wasn't careful when I lived in Hawaii. I surfed every chance I got. Sat on my surfboard with my thighs baking in the sun. For hours. No sunscreen. I…I hated my thighs. I've always hated my thighs. I thought they were too fat. I despised my thighs. Now they are rebelling against me. I didn't appreciate my thighs. I took them for granted. I—"

"Stop, Donna! Stop this now. This is not helping you," Joan insisted.

Joan had managed my office for seven years, and she was a rock. Eleven years older than me, Joan had raised four girls and then her granddaughter. I needed her calmness. There was a prolonged pause before she said, "The medical world has made giant steps concerning cancer. You're going to be fine. You know how to handle this. Focus on healing, not the disease."

"What? What are you saying?"

"Visualize your own healing. Take a warm bath, light a candle, and meditate."

"Are you insane?" I barked back. "I can't."

"You have to rid yourself of doubt and believe you'll be okay. You're getting worked up before you have all the facts."

"Facts? What facts do I need? It's melanoma! It's cancer!"

"You have to schedule a doctor's appointment," she stated adamantly.

"I called San Francisco, but all I got was a recording. They closed before calling me back. Now it's the weekend." My voice croaked, "I can't wait. I am jumping out of my skin."

"I don't want to lecture you about what you should or shouldn't do, but you have a doctor who knows about treatment. You have a child to raise, friends who adore you, and the rest of your life to live. You have to fight this. If you don't, no one else will." She paused a moment. "Are you going to be all right tonight? Do you want me to come over and stay with you?"

Joan's granddaughter had driven from Los Angeles and was visiting for a few days and I knew they were excited about spending time together, but I couldn't trust myself to be alone right now. "I hate to ask for help. But I'm scared."

"I'll be there within the hour. Meantime, calm down, pull yourself together, and tuck Mariah in bed. It's not good for her to see you like this. Can you do that?"

"Yes. I think so."

Walking into the bathroom, I doused my face with cold water.

Entering the living room, I found Mariah focused on the TV. "Mommy, I feel a little better. I'm watching a funny show."

Sheba glanced at me, and I could see her eyes had some of her lively sparkle back. Her medicine must be working. Swallowing the lump in my throat, I forced myself to sound upbeat. "I'll be right back, and then we're going to get you ready for bed." I rushed into the bathroom, closed the door harder than I intended, and turned on the water. Frigid water gushed from the faucet. I dampened a washcloth and laid it against my face. Waves of nausea churned my stomach. Retching into the toilet, spent, I finally collapsed on the cool floor tile. *Need to get Mariah into bed. Keep a normal schedule. Joan will be here soon. Get a grip.* I dabbed at my face with a washcloth and rinsed my mouth.

Grabbing Mariah's and Sheba's medicine from the kitchen counter, I returned to the living room. Minutes later, Mariah was protesting as I prepared to dose her with medicine while she sat on the couch with her fluffy sister. "Mommy, I don't like the taste. Do I have to take it?"

"If you want to feel better you do." I patted Sheba's head. "Sheba took her medicine like a good girl." *Thank heavens I caught the cat before she ran away and hid. Why can't I take medicine to make the cancer disappear? A spoonful of something and zip. Gone.*

"Let's pass on the Big Bird bedtime story tonight. I promise to read more pages tomorrow night," I said with a shaky voice as I held my daughter's hand and walked down the hall toward her bedroom.

"Oh, okay, but promise," Mariah whined. "Are you okay? You look sick."

Mumbling, I whispered, "I don't know. Maybe I have what you and Sheba have."

Mariah dropped her clothes on the floor and put on her pink zebra-striped pajamas. Tucking my daughter in, I pulled up her comforter. "I love you. You know that," I said, hearing desperation in my voice.

"I love you too," she said softly.

Amazing. My first grader loved me too; this is how I imagined it would be. What I never thought was that I would have cancer. I was boiling up like an overheated nuclear reactor, as close to the edge of a meltdown as a mom could be. "Goodnight, Mariah."

"Mommy. I can't go to sleep yet."

"Yes, you can." Hoping I could keep it together until I left her room.

"Have to say my five positive self-talks or I can't go to sleep."

"Sorry. Almost forgot. Let me hear them."

"I am happy. I am smart. I am a good friend." Pausing for a moment, she continued, "I love Sheba. I love my Mommy."

Clearing the lump in my throat, I weakly said, "Sleep tight. Kisses. You're the best."

"Hugs back to you," she said in a tiny voice.

Sheba, sitting in the hall outside Mariah's bedroom, glanced at me. Lifting her up, I cuddled her to my heart. "I love you too. Staying here with you and Mariah means more to me than anything on Earth." *Please, let me live.*

Joan arrived at my house within the hour wearing blue flannel pajamas beneath her goose-down hooded parka. I interpreted it as a sign that she had considered the possibility of a long night. She took one look at me, sighed, and sat down beside me on the sofa. A writer by trade, she combed her habitually busy fingers through short brunette hair. "You look like something Sheba dragged in from the garden. What do you feel like doing? Do you want to talk? It helps to get it all out."

"Talk." I kept twisting the ring on my finger as I thought about what Doctor Mandell had said. "How does this happen? Getting the cancer, I mean." Almost shouting, I continued, "I don't want to talk. I want to live!"

Joan put her arm around my shoulder, saying, "I'm making you a cup of green tea and you're going to bed. Donna, try to relax. I'm staying here tonight."

After a few sips of hot tea, I obediently headed for the bedroom. Unsurprisingly, my expectations for sleep were dashed the minute I laid down. Tossing and turning, desperation shuddered my body into convulsions. Surrounded by darkness, I tried to visualize how death would be. Would I feel pain? Would it take months, or even a year? My life would come to a screeching halt. Trapped in this weekend time warp, I couldn't halt the panic challenging my rationality.

Melanoma, what did I know about it? I had heard that it was the worst form of skin cancer, caused by overexposure to the sun, and frequently fatal. My mind bounced from one emotion to another: apprehension, fear, remorse for my fun in the sun days on a surf board, and the stark realization that I should prepare for the worst.

George, you are my angel. I need big time help. Why this? Why now? Gripping the side of the bed as my body shuddered. *If you were here, George, what would you say to me? Let me see. Get happy. Yes, you would say get happy. Sorry, not exactly on my agenda tonight. What else would you say? There are no accidents. Everything happens for a reason. Once you understand your learning lesson, you can move to the next level.* George's wisdom echoed in my mind. *Understand the reason the cancer is here. What does this disease have to teach you?*

Not wanting to wake Mariah or Joan, who was sleeping in the guest room, I denied my urge to leap from my bed and run through the house screaming in terror. *Cancer. Cancer. Cancer.* I pressed my hand hard against my mouth. All that came out was a pathetic whimper, a stifled sob.

Don't focus on the problem
Focus on the solution

Unable to endure squirming in the tangled bedding a second longer, I yanked back my down comforter and stormed out into the living room. The clock read 2:13. Soothing flames flickered in the fireplace, giving the room a cozy cottage feeling. From me, it merited only a frightened glance. Wrapped up in my problems, the fire only brought cremation to mind, and the effect was tomblike. How ironic, as a motivational speaker who lectures on strategies for positive change, I was being forced to walk my talk. Face my demons.

Emotionally I was bankrupt from dealing with my mother's condition in the nursing home, the death of my father, and the tortuous probate trial. I had no reserves.

Joan entered the room yawning, her thick brown hair tousled from sleep. "Thought I heard you. Do you have anything in the house to help you sleep?"

"No! You can go back to sleep," I snapped.

"There's an old saying, 'Giving advice is a fool's errand.' How about I just listen?" She gently sat on the far side of the sofa. I sat in a ball with my knees pulled tight to my chest and my arms wrapped around them.

"Joan, I can't sleep. I can't. If you were in my shoes, what would you do?"

After a moment, she smiled, "For me, baking bread is totally therapeutic. The act of setting out all the ingredients and imagining how it will taste when they come together nurtures my spirit. The scent of baking bread fills me with comfort, like natural Valium. You ought to try it sometime."

"Me, bake bread? In this state?

She didn't answer. She only gave me a look that implied she wasn't the one who needed Doctor Phil. I moved at a snail's pace to my bedroom and attempted to sleep again. Was this the longest night in the world or what? Crawling back into bed, I plumped up the pillow and pulled at my comforter. The pounding of my heart, plus the ebb and flow of fear, kept me awake. I watched the time click away on the digital clock across the room on my tall dresser. At 6:30 AM, giving up any notion of sleep, I walked into the kitchen.

Joan was sitting sleepy-eyed at the kitchen table when I entered the room. "Would it help to talk to your family?" she asked.

I sank gingerly onto a dining room chair across from her, noticing it was still dark outside. "Maybe...yes, it might help. I'll call John. What is this—Saturday? He'll be up by this time. I would guess he's reading the newspaper about now."

Joan stood up. "I'll make you some hot tea."

My hand was shaking when I pushed in the numbers on the phone. As soon as I heard his voice, I sobbed, "Daddy. Oh, Daddy. I have cancer. It's bad. I don't know if I will live."

"Donna, calm down. What are you saying?" My stepfather John sounded alarmed.

"I have skin cancer. I'll need surgery," I moaned.

"First of all, calm yourself," he insisted. "Listen to me. It's not your time. I know for sure it is not your time."

"You don't understand, Daddy," I fretted.

"Give this old man some credit. You have a daughter to raise, a life to experience together. That little girl needs you. You are going to stay right here."

"I wanted to talk. I am so scared."

"Only natural that you are scared, but scared won't heal you or help you raise your daughter. You are a mom and you have to keep it together for that little one of yours."

"I understand, but…but it's hard."

"I know it is, but you're tough. Your mother is a fighter and so are you," John said with conviction in his voice.

I was on the verge of losing control and heading for a meltdown. "Da...Daddy, I love you. I have to hang up. I promise I will call when I know more."

"Please call me soon. You will be fine. I love you too." He paused, and then with a kindness in his voice, John said, "You have that wonderful daughter of yours to raise. Believe me when I say it is not your time."

"Thanks," I whimpered.

Joan stared back at me from across the kitchen after hearing the end of the conversation and then walked over and placed a steaming cup of tea in front of me. "Your mom being paralyzed in the nursing home must take all his energy. He visits her every day. John's plate is already full. Remember, he loves you. It might take him some time to process the information you told him. I'm sure he doesn't want to lose your mother, and now to think of you having cancer must be overwhelming. Call him back tomorrow."

I played with the tag on my teabag. "You're right."

Who was next? I should call my brother. I counted four rings before he picked up, sounding groggy and grouchy.

"Listen," I wailed between gut-wrenching, breathless gasps for air. I had worked myself into a state of extreme anxiety. "It's serious. I'm sick. I have skin cancer."

After a pause he said, "I have friends who have had skin cancer and they're still around and healthy. The doctors have all kinds of new treatments today."

Deep breath. In. Out. "This is advanced, not basal cell like most people get, but melanoma. I need surgery. It could be in my lymph nodes."

"I get the picture. I sympathize. But this isn't brain surgery. The doctors have treatments for this. Stop getting yourself all worked up. When are you going to the doctor?"

"I hope this coming week. I need to get an appointment as soon as possible. I have to find out if the cancer has spread. My doctor said I have to see a specialist right away," I blurted out.

"Call me when you have more details. Try to settle down. I'm going back to sleep. Talk to you later," he said as he hung up.

Wasn't there anyone who could understand my fears of the deadly disease? What I was going through? What was I thinking? My brother and I were on the same side during the trial and he was supportive, but he was not good at showing emotion or compassion when it came to sickness. He probably thought I was overreacting. I did have a flare for that. Hurt is how I felt. *Sure wish George were alive. He would understand. He would say the right words I need to hear.*

Abruptly I asked, "Rosella is in the states visiting from England, right? Isn't she in Seattle?"

Joan nodded. "Yes. Are you thinking of asking her to leave her friends there and come to Tahoe?"

"I sure am. She's my friend too, and a brilliant healer." I rummaged through a stack of papers on the counter. "I know I have her number here somewhere. She'll come, Joan. I know she will. I need to call her."

Joan shook her head and headed for the kitchen. "I'm making coffee."

Describing Rosella is like depicting a bird in flight. She's an old soul hiding behind a dazzling smile and knowing eyes. She's positive, vivacious, an expert at tai chi, and a dedicated spiritual writer devoted to daily meditation. We first met on a cruise ship, where I was speaking and she was working as a social director. Our friendship blossomed even though we lived worlds apart, and, somehow, every few years we managed to spend time together, an enlightened spirit I loved to hang out with. Digging out the note with her information, I spoke with an English accent as Rosella would, "I'll just ring her up."

A sleepy British voice immediately answered, "Yes. Rosella here."

"Rosella, it's Donna." Sobbing and blubbering out the events of the last fourteen hours, I continued, "Need you. I'm begging you. Please say you'll come to Tahoe. I'll buy the ticket. Really need you. Can't get through this without you!"

After an exceptionally long pause, Rosella said, "I don't know if I can."

"I know this is a change in your plans and wouldn't ask if I weren't desperate. Please!"

After another long pause, Rosella said, "Right. Book the flight. I'll ask my friends to take me to the airport. It's a fair drive. I'll get you straightened out. Right. Yes. I will make some soup and we'll meditate. But I can only stay for two days."

"Thank you," I said, wiping my swollen eyes with a wet tissue.

"Right! Meantime, pull yourself together. Get ahold of your emotions. This is not helping you," my friend stated in a no-nonsense tone.

A river of tears continued as my head throbbed like a bongo drum. "I can't."

Joan walked into the room carrying a coffee mug, dark circles roosting beneath her eyes. She gave me a cursory glance.

"Pull yourself together," Rosella admonished from the other end of the line. "Listen to me right now. Stop the crying. Think what it will do to Mariah."

I wasn't so far gone that I didn't feel a stab of dismay. Normally optimistic and patient, my friend had never spoken to me so brusquely and with such harsh honesty. Stretching and rolling my shoulders back. "Rosella," I said, fearful she wouldn't come if I didn't do as she ordered, "I'll book your ticket. Flights run regularly from Seattle to Reno. Joan is here, but she hasn't had any sleep and shouldn't make the drive. I'll ask my girlfriend, Angela, to pick you up at the airport. Call you back with the details."

"Right. Meantime, this is your assignment. Meditate and sleep. Will you do that?"

"I'll give it my best shot."

Standing in the dining room. "Done, Rosella's booked. Done, Nancy's coming to relieve you, Joan. Done, Angela is picking up Rosella at the airport," I stated in an anxious, forceful tone as I began to circle the table. Stopping suddenly, I said, "Thank heavens for friends and neighbors who like me."

"That does it," Joan said, picking up the phone. "Before I leave, I'm calling Doctor Mandell to ask him for a prescription to calm you down. You cannot keep dancing on the edge like this. Mariah is going to wake up soon, and you need to take care of her."

"I can't even take care of myself. How can I take care of Mariah?"

"You're a mother. You just do it, that's all. Physically, you're perfectly capable."

I paced the house during Joan's conversation with Doctor Mandell.

"No, Doctor, Valium is not strong enough. Donna hasn't slept a wink. She needs something to knock her out. I'm leaving and the next shift is on her way over." Then I heard, "That should be fine. No, she didn't get through to the hospital in San Francisco yet, but she left a few voice messages. Yes, I'll tell her what you said." There was a long pause then Joan said, "Thank you, Doctor."

"Tell me what he said," I insisted.

"He's prescribing a sedative for you."

"I'll call Nancy again—my nurse friend. She only lives two blocks from here, and I can ask her to pick it up at the pharmacy on her way over. I know she'll do it," I said hopefully.

Joan continued, "He also said that he already called the Melanoma Center twice and could only leave a voice message. You're to keep trying first thing on Monday."

True to her word, a huge smile illuminating her face, Nancy arrived with my prescription. She filled the room with her relaxed, self-assured energy. In fact, I had never seen her lose her cool. Nancy glided into the room with her 5'8" runner's body, strawberry blonde hair, and green eyes. "Donna, Nurse Nancy is here and it is medicine time." She took one look at me and shook her head. "In a bad way."

"Yeah," I stated in a lifeless tone as I sat slumped on a dining room chair.

"Here's the deal: You are in no shape to look after Mariah, so I'll take her and she can play with my daughter. Don't worry, they'll have fun, I'll keep them busy. As a nurse and a mother, I can tell you Mariah does not need to see you in this state."

I protested, but Nancy said firmly, "Orders from me. I'm calling another one of your girlfriends to stay with you until Rosella arrives."

You get back what you give out. That is what my mentor had told me many times. Friends and community, I had given my time generously. I did it because it was the right thing to do. I wasn't looking for a payback, but now the idea of being alone terrified me. I felt blessed that my friends were concerned about me.

Mariah came running out of her bedroom, still in her pajamas. Rushing over to me, she shouted, "Mommy, Mommy, I made something to make you feel better." She gave me a handmade yellow card with little red flowers scribbled around the outside of the words she carefully printed:

Mom did you KNOW that
it is LOVE that brings us to LIFE
on Earth!
Love Mariah

I read the words out loud, choking up. "You wrote this?"

Mariah nodded and beamed. "I wrote it for you."

"This is very…" I had to clear my throat so I could continue. "Beautiful."

"I'm feeling better now. Are you?"

"I am now that I read your card." I was about to fall apart again. I had to block my doomsday thoughts before I slipped back to a place I didn't want to be. Not in front of Mariah. "How about you get a bowl of cereal?"

"I'm hungry," she said, taking my hand and pulling me toward the kitchen, Sheba hot on our heels.

Nancy, being very observant and sensing I probably couldn't hold it together for much longer, quickly said, "Don't bother. She can eat breakfast at my house." Smiling at Mariah, she said, "My daughter was just waking up when I left. Do you want to come over, have breakfast, and play with Sydney today?"

"Wow, Mommy, can I?"

"You sure can, after you take your medicine."

She was quick to swallow her liquid medicine without one complaint. Then Mariah dashed down the hall, and a few minutes later she appeared in her red winter coat and furry boots with a couple of books and a stuffed animal under her arm. "You get better. I got better. Sheba got better."

As I watched Mariah get into my girlfriend's car, I kept throwing her kisses. I wrapped my arms around me, but couldn't stop the chills that invaded my body. Would I live to raise my daughter?

Lessons Learned:

Friendship is caring

Chapter Twenty-Three
Help from Above

"Stop this fussing right now," Rosella ordered as she walked into my house and gave me a hug. She stood just shy of five feet, with brown, shoulder-length hair. Gazing at me with her passionate dark eyes, she said, "We will have none of this carrying-on."

"It has not been twenty-four hours since my diagnosis and I am giving myself one full day to grieve, cry, yell, and complain!" Glancing at the clock, I said tersely, "I have another thirty minutes." I continued to stand in the middle of the room as I stomped my foot.

Rosella heaved a sigh and threw up her hands. "Right. My job is in the kitchen. I am off to put on the kettle and make some soup."

I could hear the clatter of cabinets opening and closing and the banging of pots and pans. When I finally joined her, Rosella was singing as she stirred a large pot on the stove.

"There you are, Miss Sunshine. First on my assignment list is soup. Enough to eat and freeze. Next is meditation time and…" I balked but she continued, "I am here for two days and have some mighty fixing to do. So there will be no complaining from you."

Nothing would come out of my mouth; I only nodded.

"Good. We start with a cup of hot tea and have a chat. You can't dodge your lesson," Rosella announced.

With tough love for self-pity, Rosella managed to keep me from going insane through Saturday and Sunday. It might have taken her twenty lectures, but she made me live in the moment with her prescription of hot herbal tea, homemade soup, meditation, and sleep. Her formula was simple: eliminate fear by tuning into healing energy.

"Donna, darling," Rosella said in her British accent, "you are magnificent. You are part of the healing process."

"Whoever thought when we met on that cruise ship eight years ago that you would…?" My voice trailed off.

"Life is full of surprises." She let loose an infectious laugh and threw back her head. "I was assigned to take care of you. Right, make sure you had everything you required for your speech—you were in the right location and all your handouts were printed. Here I am taking care of you again." Rosella smiled as she rested against the kitchen counter. "This time making sure you have everything for your healing."

My lips turned up slightly as I said softly, "Sorry, looks like you have a life assignment."

Sharp-witted Rosella let out a thunderous laugh. "Oh, Lordy, what did I do to deserve this?" She grinned. "I am heading back to England and I only want to hear about your success. Do you hear me?"

"I do. I love you. Rosella, you are grand," I said, fighting back tears.

"Enough crying. Right, you think about being healthy and your daughter. Meditate! Meditate three times a day." Her voice lightened. "Always know I want the best for you."

"Thank you for your patience and encouragement. I couldn't have made it through this nerve-wracking weekend without you. "

"Nonsense!" Rosella stated.

"Well, without you, I would have had fifteen mini breakdowns."
Rosella chuckled.

The next few days I kept myself on the move, as it was the only way

I could sidestep my growing anxiety. I walked Mariah to the school bus every morning and then returned home. That's when my fears escalated. I couldn't focus on work, so I let all my phone calls go to voicemail.

My constant pacing had me wondering about my soundness of mind. I phoned the Melanoma Center six times Monday, nine times Tuesday, and faxed them as many times on both days. I did the same on Wednesday, Thursday, and Friday. I never spoke to anyone; I only left messages.

After a week with no response, I panicked. I couldn't sleep, couldn't eat. I surmised that I had been sick for longer than I thought and played over and over in my head the various signals my body had given me over the past year that I hadn't paid attention to. Always exhausted, I was constantly fighting off the flu or terrible colds, which I now realized were an indication my immune system was weak and had no resistance to combat disease.

I pondered the seeming coincidence that I had changed my routine dermatologist check-up to the end of February instead of my normal May appointment. My inner voice had kept gnawing at me to schedule a visit with the dermatologist, the thought recurring night after night like a dream until I finally heeded it and made the early appointment.

My mentor had insisted that even when something didn't make sense, I should always trust my intuition. *Thanks, George, for your lecture after lecture to act on my gut feeling.*

I was only able to pull myself together for a few hours when Mariah was home with me. I wished Sara hadn't moved back to New Zealand—I certainly could have used her help now.

Doctor Mandell called me at the end of the week to inform me he hadn't been able to talk to anyone at UC San Francisco either. He kept stressing how important timing was to my case, and to keep calling. His forecast rumbled through my head like thunder in the distance. "If this cancer spreads to the lymph nodes, it is life threatening."

Each passing day, the tension increased, cramping my shoulders and neck. Another girlfriend of mine had Mariah over to hang out with her daughter on the weekend, realizing I was in no shape to entertain my own child. I still could hardly eat.

The next week started as I agonized over my dismal situation. I walked Mariah to the school bus, hoping to keep up the appearance of a normal routine. Next, I followed up with a barrage of phone calls to the Melanoma Center. No call back. Tuesday I did the same. At home alone, my behavior became erratic—one second I'd be standing, the next slumped on the sofa, and then I'd carry on my pacing and stop abruptly, staring at the phone, demanding it to ring.

"What should I do?" I screamed as loud as I could to my living room ceiling. I continued to gaze upward as the words spilled out before I realized I was saying them. "Father, I know you were there for me during the probate trial. It was exhausting...physically. Now I have cancer. Overexposure to the sun. I surfed up a storm in Hawaii and didn't wear sunscreen. That's part of the reason. But Doug and I went through hell during probate. I had so much stress during that time… result, cancer. Can't even get an appointment to see if they can help me. Be the great salesman you always were. Please, get to work. I need an appointment at UC San Francisco Melanoma Center right away," I stated with conviction. "I want someone from that place to return my phone calls. Get me an appointment now!" Wheezing from the outburst, I clutched my chest, rocking back and forth, straining to pull myself together while battling against mounting fear. *How pitiful is this? Get a grip, Donna.*

Rosella's last words as she left were compelling. "Meditate, meditate three times a day." I hadn't been able to do it once. Maybe the time was now. *All right already, Rosella.*

Mariah was out of her bath, hair dry, in her pajamas and listening to music in her bedroom as she twirled around and danced. I stole a quick glance so as not to disturb her. Sheba lay in the middle of the bedroom doorway, watching her too.

Dimming the lights in the living room, I burned a scented white candle and snuggled under a blanket in my oversized chair with large armrests. I straightened my back and rotated my neck to alleviate the pressure I felt in my body. *Focus. Breathe deeply.* Turning on soft flute music with a remote, I imagined the tension leaving my feet, moving up to my legs, torso, chest, shoulders, and arms. I wiggled my fingers, opening and closing them. Rubbing my temples, I believed I could feel the tightness lessening. I gently placed my hands on my lap with palms open and upward as my mind drifted with the music. *Breathe in and breathe out. Breathe in and breathe out. Breathe in and breathe out.*

I wouldn't say I was completely relaxed, but at least I was breathing longer and gentler breaths instead of choppy ones. I sat still in the same place for at least fifteen minutes. Unexpectedly, my state was interrupted by the phone. It took me a few seconds to center my thoughts and get up. The clock on the wall read 6:55 PM.

Feeling my throat constrict, I answered, "Hello."

"Is this Donna Hartley?" the woman at the other end questioned.

"Yes. This is Donna. Who's calling?"

"I'm with the UC San Francisco Melanoma Center. I've heard your many messages and seen your faxes. Your last fax kept falling from the pile. I must have picked it up off the floor at least three times in the last hour."

I thought I detected a hint of irritation, but I said nothing. I was just pleased someone had finally returned my phone messages.

She switched her tone and became very professional. "I'm calling because we have an appointment for you. Are you available next Monday morning? It would be an all-day evaluation."

"Available. Yes!" I said, feeling a rush of relief. "Yes, I am."

"You'll be seeing Doctor Kashani, our co-director. He's extremely qualified."

"Thank you. Thank you." I exhaled, like I had been holding my breath.

"Please be here one hour prior to your appointment. That would be nine o'clock Monday morning. Go directly to the reception desk and pick up your request for blood work and x-rays. Can you be here by then?"

"Yes. Of course. I'll be there on time," I said with certainty.

"Then we'll see you next Monday. Let me give you the exact address."

As the woman spoke, I wrote down the details.

Feeling immensely grateful, I ran to the photo of my father that hung on the wall. *I'm not sure how this works, but my mentor told me many times I could ask for help. George was emphatic that no one can intervene from the spirit side unless specifically asked. I needed your assistance and got it...an appointment. Thank you.* I inhaled deeply. *I know what I am supposed to do...meditate and, yes, meditate some more.*

A tingling sensation vibrated in my body; I sensed that George was telling me to get ready to see the doctor. What had Mr. Miracle Man said to me in one of his blooming Georgeisms? "Believe in the outcome. Get ready for it to happen. Be prepared and the success you want will follow."

"George, George, oh dear George, I will do it." I burst out laughing because I could imagine him saying, "Well, it's about time! You were hell-bent for leather on giving me a hard time when I was alive."

Rushing to my nightstand, I pulled out the envelope that contained the gift of intuition that George had bestowed on me years before during his last visit to Lake Tahoe and read the section on calming the mind and listening for the answers.

Meditation

Meditation is a calm state of relaxation that creates spiritual and physical well-being. Begin by meditating three times a week for ten or fifteen minutes. Once the process becomes more natural, you will want to meditate more often to help release stress and restore energy.

To begin, turn off all the distractions in your life and clear your mind. Find a comfortable chair, light a scented candle, and play soft music or a guided meditation CD. Close your eyes, breathe deeply, relax your body, and let the calmness settle over you.

Meditation is soul-searching reflection to help you reach within and bring harmony and healing into your life. Meditation promotes intuition and attracts the knowing to help you make better decisions. When you pray, you ask for help, and when you meditate, you receive the answers. Meditate often because it heightens your total awareness and spiritual enlightenment.

AFFIRMATION:
I meditate for inner peace and wisdom.

Sheba plopped on my lap and gently moved to my left thigh, exactly where the doctor had performed the biopsy. She turned around a few times, then snuggled in, purring. I stared at her. Sheba had never sat just on my left thigh before. She knew. Sheba understood. *Let's get this healing started.*

Lesson Learned:

Live in the moment

Chapter Twenty-Four

Why Me?

I'm strong. I can handle this! I can go to the doctor's appointment on my own.

"Donna, let me take you to your cancer specialist in San Francisco. I've been through this." Teresa's voice grew gentler over the phone. "You need support. Understand that when I was diagnosed with breast cancer, my husband was by my side."

"Teresa, I'm fine," I said as I walked in circles around my living room.

"Please think about it. I'm leaving that day open, and if you change your mind, call."

"Really, I'll be okay," I tried to say convincingly. The reality was that I didn't like asking for help. I learned early in my life that I had to make decisions on my own. I always considered myself weak if I needed support, but I didn't say that to Teresa.

"Call. I'll be there for you." Teresa's voice echoed kindness.

"I've gone to most all my doctor's appointments alone so don't worry, but thank you so much for thinking of me. It's generous of you to offer to drive all the way to San Francisco and back, but you have two daughters to look after."

"Don't worry about me—my husband can take care of the girls for one day. I'm concerned about you," Teresa said. "By the way, do you have someone to take care of Mariah?"

"Yes, Cathee will look after her since her daughter is in Mariah's first grade class. Well, for that matter, so is your daughter." I paused. "You know, I am grateful to have so many friends in this small community. Really, I am."

Even with supportive friends, the nights were the worst. I couldn't sleep and I tossed and turned, sweating one second only to wrap myself up again, freezing, five minutes later. My mind conjured up worries, always with the concern of what would happen to my daughter. Here I was, an inspirational speaker, focusing on managing change, and I wasn't dealing with it well at all. I thought I would be okay, but I was a mess. I understood the way I was raised; with the back-and-forth between battling parents, I became responsible for my life early on. Would it be better if my girlfriend took me to the doctor? Did I now have to learn how to ask for help? What was my lesson? I knew there was a spiritual message in the chaos of what was going on in my life, but the concept was foggy in my head. *Lesson, lesson. What do I need to learn to understand?* I asked myself countless times during those sleepless nights.

Just after dawn the day after I received the call from Teresa, I phoned her and asked if she would still go to the doctor's appointment with me in two days. I felt needy asking, but my nerves were so rattled and my fears were accelerating. I was starting to become aware that I was incapable of handling the travel and medical exam by myself. What if the doctor said the cancer had spread already?

Teresa didn't hesitate. "Sure. I'll be at your house first thing in the morning, 5 AM, and we can drive together," she said like we were going shopping in the city, but I knew she comprehended the seriousness of the appointment since her surgery was still raw in her mind. I chuckled because she was doing everything in her power to be supportive. Teresa was exactly who I needed to help me through the uncertainly I was facing.

After I hung up with Teresa, the truth of my situation slammed me in the chest: In only two days, the specialist would give me my diagnosis. I crossed my arms and clutched my elbows. Would I live to raise my daughter?

Right on time, I stood, petrified, beneath the imposing arch above the main entrance to the UCSF Melanoma Center, staring through the glass doors. This couldn't be happening. To other people, yes, but cancer was never part of my program.

Strangely, the drive to San Francisco had seemed like any other trip to the city, but standing here now, I realized it wasn't. This journey would deliver a massive decision about my future.

Teresa nudged my arm. "Come on, Donna, let's find the reception desk."

Understanding my paralysis, she took my arm and gently guided me toward the door.

Glancing at the thirty-something, slender, and petite blonde beside me, I was grateful for her company. Teresa had a take-charge attitude and a sensible head on her shoulders. I admired how she radiated confidence. She had been down this road and conquered her disease and now was a beacon of light for me.

As we entered, I said, "This lobby is so...so imposing."

"I'm right here with you. Don't worry." She swiveled her head, then pointed. "Reception is over there."

The receptionist was skilled in grilling patients and expediting paperwork necessary to maneuver the gravely ill to their destinations. When the interrogation ended, I was handed a stack of papers and directed down the hall. "X-ray," she said more sharply than I'm sure she intended, "is on the second floor. Next."

Walking in the corridor, when it came time to turn right, my mind went blank.

As I stalled, concern blanketed Teresa's face. "Are you all right?"

"I...I don't understand what's happening," I said, panic seizing my chest. "I can't tell which way is right."

Teresa slipped her hand under my arm and steered me to the right. "This way, sister."

I kept mum until we reached the entrance to the lab. "Thank you. If not for you, I'd still be stuck in the hall trying to figure out the left from the right."

I graced the lab with five vials of my blood. Teresa again took hold of my arm and we shuffled off to x-ray. Normally I had an abundance of energy, but not today.

Waiting my turn kept my nerves on edge. After I was checked in and completed the paperwork, I was handed a smock with teddy bears on it. I was far too old to be clothed in colorful baby animals, but who was I to grumble? As I submitted myself to views of my chest and back, I wondered if the technician knew something I didn't. Walking out the door, I asked Teresa, "Why did they take x-rays of my back and chest? The cancer is in my leg."

"I'm sure it's your doctor being thorough. From what I've gathered, he's well-respected here. Probably making sure all the bases are covered, wants to have a full report," Teresa said, peeking at her watch. "Oh my gosh. It's time for your appointment already."

The waiting room was extremely spacious, but the disturbing fact was that every seat was occupied. No laughter or light chatter, only somber faces. Waves of fear gripped my stomach. Three women behind the counter were actively attending to patients as I waited in line to hand over my insurance information in exchange for the usual clipboard with yet more forms to be filled out.

"When you have completed your paperwork, please return them to the desk," the efficient receptionist said, only glancing at me for a second.

"New patient lowdown," Teresa stated with a grin. "I remember it well. They want to know everything about you, going back five generations."

She picked up a magazine as I began my assignment. Concentrating on the task proved to be more difficult than I expected. I was distracted by the goings-on around me. I didn't necessarily want to get up-close and personal, but nevertheless I found myself checking out the other patients. It was hard not to. Was it always this busy on "New Patient Monday?"

Back in Tahoe, Doctor Mandell had told me a patient had to have advanced melanoma, like me, to warrant an appointment here. The Melanoma Center had an excellent reputation and a successful survival rate for its patients. I thought, *This is why it took scheduling so long to call me back.* This place was jammed with patients, with another seven waiting in line to fill out their medical forms. As the nurse called out names, solemn-faced people walked slowly from the reception area. I couldn't help but notice how no one leapt up in eagerness.

My hand clutched my chest when I saw her, a beautiful and obviously pregnant young woman with long brown hair. A man I assumed to be her husband held her hand and was reassuring her. Teresa patted my arm, and I knew she had seen the woman too. I glanced at her and shook my head, feeling my heart accelerate. I felt terrified for my daughter. *Don't go there. There's no way to make sense of all this or predict the outcome. Focus on the now.*

The paperwork was extensive beyond belief, with family history and my complete medical background. The only medication I was taking was for my hormones. The drugs balanced my hot flashes and probably kept me somewhat rational. After handing the clipboard back, I extracted a brochure from a pile on the table.

Scanning the pamphlet, I reread the words on the front again to make sure I had read them right. "One out of seven children born today will develop skin cancer." The statistics were shocking. Would I be around to see that my own daughter applied sun block? How did my girlfriend sitting next to me deal with her breast cancer and the thought of not being alive to raise her children?

"Donna Hartley."

I jerked when I heard my name and gasped. "This is it." Turning to Teresa, I grabbed her arm. "My turn."

Lesson Learned:

Have inner strength

Chapter Twenty-Five
Challenging the Prognosis

Wearing a hospital gown, this one patterned with little pink flowers, I sat on the exam table, bare feet dangling, as the nurse took my blood pressure and temperature. *Get on with it! My blood pressure has always been on the low side, so it's fine. I don't have a fever either. I have cancer. I* was angry this procedure was taking so long. I was scared, no, terrified. Ordered to the scale, I rolled my eyes at Teresa. She winked back.

Shocked when the number registered, I said, "Found something good in all of this; I've lost twelve pounds! I'm at my Miss Hawaii weight, and it's been some time since I've seen this number." *An outrageous price to pay for weight loss.*

When the nurse left the room, Teresa stood and said, "Be right back. Need a bathroom."

For the first time that day, I was alone. Sitting on the scratchy paper, I appraised my surroundings. Nothing intimidating: hand soap, cotton balls, sanitizer, and an anatomical poster on the wall. *Where's Teresa? What's taking her so long? Total silence. Scary. Where is she?* I wiggled my toes to get warmth back into my feet. My next distraction to occupy my mind with anything, but worry was counting the square titles on the floor. *What could be keeping her? She should be back by now.*

The door opened. "Teresa! What took you so long?" I blurted out

"This is one big place, but they don't have near enough bathrooms." She looked directly at me. "Are you okay?"

"I...was scared. I was...afraid."

"Don't worry." She moved near me and held my hand. "I understand."

"I'm sorry I'm being so...." Water blurred my eyes and I couldn't talk.

"It's all right. It's normal to feel this way." Changing the subject, Teresa continued, "From my own experience, I can coach you on what questions to ask and write everything down. Would you like me to do that?"

"I think I can handle most of the questions, but if I forget something important, please jump right in. Nervous as I am, I'm afraid I won't remember much. I'd appreciate it if you could take notes."

Seconds later, the door opened and not one, but a team of three doctors entered the tiny exam room. A well-dressed man in his early forties with a dark complexion and a friendly smile introduced himself and shook my hand. "I am Doctor Kashani. The team and I are here to evaluate your condition and assess the best method of treatment. You will be examined by each of us."

I nodded at the young female and the white-haired gentleman as they introduced themselves. I heard their names, but they went right out of my brain as quickly as they went in. Too much to think about. Thank heavens Teresa jumped right in and introduced herself. I couldn't even think about proper etiquette and introductions.

Inch by inch. I had never been examined so thoroughly, and certainly never between my toes and every part of my scalp. They scrutinized and conferred on every suspicious spot and blemish, and each one was noted in my file.

Doctor Kashani addressed me directly. "May I call you Donna?"

"Yes."

"From the look of your skin, you have spent extensive time in the sun."

"Yes," I squeaked out. Clearing my throat I continued, "My heritage is mostly Irish. I'm from Pennsylvania. But I went to college in Hawaii and spent five years surfing."

"That accounts for the sun damage."

The fact that he didn't lecture or fault me for years of frying my body helped calm my raw nerves. *What was done was done. Fix it.* Doctor Kashani didn't mince words, but rather, carefully chose them. Teresa bobbed her head at me more than once during the conversation, signaling she was impressed.

"Our team will consult to discuss the best method of treatment for you. I'll ask that you and Teresa have a seat in the waiting room. We've scheduled a psychologist appointment for you next. Afterwards, we'll meet again. I'll see you later," Doctor Kashani said as the team vacated the room.

Psychologist. So now I am officially crazy. I need a shrink? Did everyone see the psychologist or only a few select nutty patients, like me? Did the doctors already know something about my condition that would cause them to make me visit the shrink before they informed me of my situation? I made up my mind I wasn't going into the psychiatrist's office alone. Teresa had been through the whole nine yards with me, and I wasn't about to hide anything from her now.

Summoned from the waiting room, I said to the man standing with my file, "I'd like my friend to come with me. Anything I have to say, she can hear."

Waiting for the psychologist to review my files, my girlfriend and I settled in on the traditional comfy couch. He was the same man who had called my name in the waiting room. The longer I sat, the more impatient I became.

The psychologist's lightly graying hair, metal-frame glasses, preppy, pinstriped shirt, and color-matching tie gave him the appearance of a professional who was in charge. He periodically looked up to squint at me and then continued reading my file. My mind scrambled to remember his name when he introduced himself. Andrew Kni...Knei... I couldn't recall it, but as we made our way to his office, he did say he was a psychological consultant for UCSF/Mount Zion Melanoma Center.

Okay! I wanted to break the silence and scream at him. *Give it to me straight. Cut to the chase.*

The psychologist cleared his throat and began, "From Doctor Kashani's notes, your melanoma is advanced and requires surgery. We have learned patients do better when we discuss your psychological state and some of the treatments and options available to fight your disease. I see you're from Lake Tahoe. Your team may recommend ongoing treatment. Could you remain in San Francisco if you need prolonged follow-up therapy after surgery?"

What do you mean prolonged treatment? Is the cancer that bad? In a voice barely above a whisper, I choked out, "I could make arrangements... I mean I can...my brother lives near San Francisco."

"There are some cutting-edge procedures you are a good candidate for. Of course, the method of treatment depends on whether the cancer has spread to the lymph nodes. You will undergo surgery to determine that. As one of the doctors on your team, it's important I know what feelings you have regarding your impending surgery and if you are willing to consider any further treatment afterwards." He paused to squint at me again, his glasses partway down his nose. "Some people respond well to treatment, others do not."

You mean, they die. I wanted him to stop mealy-mouthing and tell me if he believed the cancer was in my lymph nodes or not. I sat silently. In a way, I wanted to withhold, to prevent him from tampering with my personal intention to beat the "Big C."

Finally, to break the silence, Teresa spoke. "You may not know Donna, but I do. You have a survivor here."

That was exactly what I needed to hear. Taking a deep inhale, I began quietly and then got louder. "I...I am a single mom with a daughter to raise. She is only six. I love my daughter." I swallowed, trying to compose myself as tears welled in my eyes. "As a child, I overcame malnutrition and underwent a heart procedure. While living in Los Angeles, I was the last survivor from my section in a DC-10 plane crash. By the way, I was Miss Hawaii and it took me five tries to win. Oh, and I practice meditation to help me focus. Where I live in Tahoe, I have a great support group of friends too." I shot a quick glance at Teresa. "And now that I have…it, I intend to do whatever I need to beat it!"

During this time, the doctor was furiously scribbling notes. When he looked up, he actually smiled. "Good. That gives me adequate information about your state of mind."

No one, including you, doc, has the right to tell me how I will handle this disease. You are probably going out to dinner with your wife tonight, and I intend to have plenty of meals with my daughter too. Listening to myself talk, I understood more clearly than ever that I was a fighter — yes, a warrior, ready to do battle and win!

In the overcrowded reception room again, waiting for my appointment with Dr. Kashani and the other doctors, I turned to my girlfriend. "Tell me how you handled all this? The cancer? Your husband? Your daughters?"

She shrugged and said, "It's different for everybody, but once you have been diagnosed with cancer, something occurs. I was afraid at first, but ultimately, I ended up exchanging my fears for hope. I didn't have a team of doctors like you do, and I must say, the thoroughness of your exam was outstanding." She giggled. "In fact, I felt like ripping off my clothes and having them check me out to make sure I don't have skin cancer."

"Teresa, that's ludicrous."

"Yes and no. I've become more vigilant of my own health. Not paranoid, but observant."

"That's what I admire about you. I would never describe you as passive."

"I could have completely shut down if my husband hadn't been right there with me, gathering the information." She paused, immersed in recalling her difficult times. "What I want to say is, I have been down the same dark road as you. I had days where I didn't...couldn't talk to anyone because the power of my own fear and the possibility of dying so young overwhelmed me. I thought about the future of my daughters all the time. At least one member of my family was always with me until I got through the worst of it." Changing the topic and focusing on me, she continued, "You'll be around to raise Mariah, because from what I've seen here, you have experienced doctors."

I felt a pang. "I'm sorry, Teresa, that I didn't understand what you were going through. I wish I would have been there for you."

"You understand now. You can be supportive when friends need you."

I glanced around the room, wall-to-wall patients from the reception desk and back to the pile of pamphlets. My throat constricted as a hemmed-in feeling descended over me like a shroud. My heart beat rapidly as I imagined what might come next.

As if reading my mind, Teresa said, "You're doing great. All this information, and the exam, it's a lot for one person, but you're right on track."

"Donna Hartley," a nurse with a clipboard announced.

My heartbeat accelerated with every step I took in the direction of the exam room.

Once inside, I glanced around the room. Only Dr. Kashani, his face radiating kindness, was there, sitting with papers spread out around him at a small table. Where were the other doctors? Was this a good or bad sign? I didn't know, but I'm sure the doctor could hear my heart beating since it sounded to me like a thunderous drumbeat in my brain. *Thump thump thump.* And it continued to grow louder.

"Please take a seat," Dr. Kashani spoke gently in a faintly accented voice.

I gingerly took a seat across from him, and Teresa sat discreetly behind me, to my right.

Dr. Kashani remarked, "I am going to explain our specific plan of action and—"

"Do you have children?" I blurted out before he could finish, apprehension crashing through my mind. I had to connect, make him understand that I needed not just a plan of action, but to live.

He sat back in his chair, somewhat flustered, coffee-colored eyes blinking rapidly. "Well, yes, I do. Two small children."

"Do you spend time with them?"

"With my hours, it is sometimes difficult."

"You should. I have a daughter. I'm a single parent. I plan on spending a lifetime with her."

His discerning gaze said he grasped my meaning. Doctor Kashani began explaining how deep the melanoma had penetrated my thigh, and the possibility of it traveling into my lymph nodes. I found myself listening, but his words jumbled in my brain. I was not capable of understanding what he was saying. Why did I have cancer? What was this disease supposed to teach me? I knew there was a spiritual purpose to this awful disease—what was it? Heal with my family, yes, I was doing that. Heal with... My brain settled for a moment. I had never considered this, but I was part of my family. I had to heal with me.

Dr. Kashani was moving forward, methodically explaining what the surgery would entail. "We will perform three procedures. The first procedure is to inject nuclear dye into the area of your cancer. The dye will register on a computer when it reaches the nearest lymph nodes. Next, we will incise and remove an area in and around the melanoma. The third procedure involves removing the lymph nodes closest to your melanoma. We send them to a lab for biopsy evaluation. The findings will provide us with the information for your course of treatment."

All I could do was nod. As an international speaker, I presented before thousands of people without fear. Now I couldn't even muster up one word.

"From your paperwork, I see you have a heart murmur. Before we do surgery, or give you anesthesia, I have written orders for a full work-up on your heart. We don't want surprises. Can you see a cardiologist?"

"Y...yes," I managed to sputter out.

"Then here are my written orders for the cardiologist and the information for your appointment with the surgeon this afternoon. Doctor Allen is located in the building across the street. He's part of our team and an excellent surgeon." He glanced at his watch. "You'll have time for lunch beforehand."

"I appreciate...thank you."

When he left the room Teresa reiterated. "You're in good hands. Let's go eat."

"I would love to get out of this building, but eat, I don't know." I forced a weak smile. "It's like my brain can't take in all these details."

I am alive. I have cancer. The doctors are going to do surgery to see if they can save me. Somehow, I needed to be part of the saving me process, too.

My gal friend rose and said, "Outside we go. I could use some of that salty San Francisco air, and I believe the sun is out. Sunshine will do your spirit wonders. I'm famished besides."

An hour later, as we entered the surgeon's office, the tension in the room was palpable. The patients, regardless of age, gender, or race, had a common concern besides going under the knife...the outcome of their surgery. *This is only another exam. You need more facts. Think of a positive outcome. You are a fighter.*

Once again I undressed and donned another short, unbecoming gown, this one with multi-colored dots. Looking at Teresa, I said, "Maybe my next career is designing a decent hospital gown."

A gentleman of impressive size wearing a crisp white coat entered the room with a pair of half-glasses positioned on his sizeable nose. Abruptly he said, "I am Doctor Allen," as he studied my chart. The intensity of the man filled the room. When he finished, he glanced at me. "I have met with the tumor doctors. Let's have a look at your thigh."

Tumor doctors—what does that mean?

During the examination, Doctor Allen uttered several unintelligible grunts. I tossed Teresa a perplexed look. His mannerisms made me feel awkward and I clamped my jaw shut. He certainly wasn't giving off the impression of excellence that Doctor Kashani had alluded to earlier. Since we had no conversation going, I stared at the medical degrees plastering every available wall space. Finally, unable to contain myself, I naively asked, "How many melanoma surgeries have you performed... similar to mine, I mean?"

He pushed up his glasses and said, "Look, I've read everything in your chart. You had malnutrition, heart catheterization at sixteen, you survived a plane crash, and you're a single mother of a young daughter. I understand why you have many reasons to live. What I do, I do well. I operate only on advanced melanoma patients and I'm extremely successful. I have developed many of the techniques that I and other surgeons use today."

Then Doctor Allen laid his massive hand on top of mine and said, "This is where you need to trust me, Donna. I meet with patients one day a week and I'm in surgery the other four. I'm confident. You should be also. You can get dressed now. On the way out, see my receptionist. She'll schedule your surgery."

When he left I looked at Teresa for some kind of support. Slowly she said, "Look at these degrees on the wall and all the articles he has written. He knows what he is doing. Not much bedside manner, but then again, he is in surgery four days a week."

I blurted out, "Right, he doesn't have to talk to his patients. They're knocked out."

My chest tightened when the receptionist informed me of my surgery date. "We can schedule your surgery in late April," the pleasant voice behind a wide smile said.

April? It's only the tenth of March. I could be dead by that time. "I can't wait that long." Panic caught in my throat.

She rechecked her calendar. "No availability."'

This was unacceptable. I had to ignore this setback and think about another option. "There will be a cancellation. My name is Donna Hartley, it is right here on my form. Please call me."

The receptionist only glared at me, saying nothing.

"Please call me when there is a cancellation. Donna Hartley."

Teresa said nothing, didn't move, only stood close beside me.

The receptionist must have had quite a bit of experience with panicky patients, because she calmly replied, "I'll look over the schedule, and if there is an opening I will call you."

The message I'd gotten today was obvious. If the cancer spread to my lymph nodes, there would be no choice but to get my affairs in order. *I need an appointment, pronto.*

Ten minutes later, we were in the car heading back to Tahoe. My girlfriend had offered to drive, but having my hands on the steering wheel would keep my mind from drifting to the negative. I glanced at her. "I had no idea cancer instills such fear and helplessness. Really, I am sorry I wasn't there for you when you went through breast cancer."

Teresa looked at me for a moment as she realigned her body in the car seat "My husband was there. Even when I lost my hair, he told me every day how beautiful I was. You don't need to apologize. Be there for someone when they need support. That's how it works."

I chuckled. "You sound like my master teacher, George. I would ask him what I could do for him. He replied, 'Be there for someone when they need a guiding hand. That's how it works.'" I would have to send a message to that angel tonight. Let him know that he was on fulltime duty watching over me to make sure I survived this disease. I had a daughter to... Oh my gosh!

"What is it?" Teresa asked sounding concerned.

"Mariah is my reason for living. She is my purpose. That's why she's in my life now. I waited seven years with eleven attempts at adoption. I understand now why it took so long. She had to be in my life at this very moment so I would fight this disease."

Teresa softly confirmed, "She is your reason for living." She emphasized the word *is*.

Crossing over the impressive Golden Gate Bridge, I glanced out at the turbulent blue water and the expansive horizon while pondering the events of the day. *Now that the doctors have teamed up to devise a plan of action, what is my role in all this? What should I do next?*

When you're sick and tired
of being sick and tired
you'll change

Lesson Learned:

Be proactive with your health

Chapter Twenty-Six

The Perfect Plan

My eyes fluttered open to dim light and the shrill ringing of the phone.

A chipper voice at the other end said, "Donna, Jeanne here. Sorry if I woke you."

"Hi, I'm not getting up early these days. Feel like I am fighting the flu. When I think about it, I have been sick more this year than usual. I'm weak."

"Understandable." She paused for a moment. "I'm anxious to hear what happened yesterday. I've been thinking about you and have come up with some ideas," she stated with enthusiasm.

Couldn't help thinking how Jeanne and George had similar traits, positive people always searching for solutions. Jeanne was the only other female, besides me, of the twelve earthly souls assigned to George. His assignment was to assist us on our spiritual journey. George had informed me that I was more trouble than all the other people put together. I always thought he was kidding, but now I don't think so. Jeanne and I had become friends, thanks to George. She had a generous nature, a larger-than-life personality, and was always there for me as a wonderful listener. If I had to describe her in one word it would be...giver.

When I didn't reply, Jeanne asked, "What did the doctor say?"

"Doctor...there were many doctors. They said the best decision for me was to have surgery as soon as possible. First they will shoot nuclear dye into my thigh where the cancer is so they can locate the nearest lymph nodes. Then the surgeon will remove tissue from in and around the melanoma area. Finally, the surgeon will operate and remove a few lymph nodes and then perform a biopsy to determine if the cancer has spread throughout my body."

"When does this happen?"

"That's the problem. Here it is, the eleventh of March, and their first opening is late April. I have to get an appointment like...today. Doctor Mandell keeps stressing how invasive this disease is and that nothing will slow it down or stop it faster than surgery. There are four stages, and if I understand this correctly, I am three. I'm worried." I squeezed my eyes shut against a fresh assault of tears.

"You are draining your energy. There's a more creative way to turn this around."

"What?"

"You tell people in your speeches that worrying doesn't solve the problem. Don't say anything, because I've been to your presentations. Well, now you have the chance to live what you teach, or walk your talk, as George would say," Jeanne insisted. "I am here to be your support."

We both fell silent for a moment. Finally, I admitted, "It's hard." Gathering my thoughts I continued, "Action is the word I use."

"Good. Let's get to work. Action it is. For starters, I want you to manage your thoughts. All the time."

"I don't know. That's practical for some problems, like your job, your house, or money issues, but cancer is unparalleled," I blurted out.

"Exactly why you need to do what I'm asking. The mind is a powerful ally and you, and only you, are in charge of your thoughts," Jeanne declared. "I want you to include this mantra in your thoughts at least two dozen times a day."

Perfect health
Perfect surgery
Perfect recovery

I was listening, but nothing seemed to sink in. I was already feeling tired again and I had only just woken up. "But Jeanne—" I started to protest.

"What you think is what you draw to yourself. How many times did George say that to us? Now, let me hear you say the perfect mantra."

"Okay. Perfect health. Perfect surgery." I paused to remember the next statement. "Perfect recovery."

"Excellent," Jeanne encouraged me. "Every time you're fearful, I want you to stop what you're doing and say this perfect mantra. Make it as automatic as breathing. Write it down on sticky notes and attach them to your mirror, refrigerator, everywhere you can see them. You're not a victim, Donna, you're a survivor. You've survived a plane crash and you can beat cancer. You have no time to waste, this is critical to your healing."

"You're right. I teach this but...it's different when it's the 'Big C.'"

"No it is not. Now say it again."

Slowly, I spoke the words, "Perfect health. Perfect surgery. Perfect recovery."

"Now say it again like you mean it, with energy and commitment, like it's already true."

I was distracted for a moment by a strong gust of wind that made a whistling sound. Looking outside, the pine trees caught my eye, standing tall against the wind and turbulent winter. I needed to stand erect with the belief that I too could withstand the storm.

Centering my attention back on the phone, I interjected, "You've heard too many of my speeches. You are starting to sound like me."

Jeanne laughed. "We all know what we are supposed to do, but sometimes we need a little direction."

She was insightful. She understood the ways demons could breed fear in a person, and she was preparing me to wage war against them.

"Don't give anyone cause to think anything negative about you. Think positive, beam a smile, even if you are scared. Say the six all-powerful words. Tell your friends about the perfect mantra. Ask them to say or think it. Feel confident about yourself."

"I think...but at night it is..."

"Daunting. I understand. But when you're depressed, you lose your connection to God. Take charge. No negative thoughts allowed. Live in the moment. This technique has your name on it. Say it again. Do it for yourself and your daughter."

"Perfect health! Perfect surgery! Perfect recovery!"

"That is a terrific start."

"Gracias," I replied as I heard Mariah call for me. "Oops. The kid is up. Talk to you soon."

Still running my conversation with Jeanne through my mind, I sat down on the edge of Mariah's bed and held out my arms to her.

She gave me a sleepy good morning smile and a bear hug. "Morning, Mommy."

As I held my daughter, I knew I was blessed. "Miss Beautiful, I want you to help Mommy. Could you? Mommy is going to have to spend time with the doctors. I have to get rid of this disease. I need your support." *Believe like a child*, I thought. I wanted to tell Mariah some details but didn't want to scare her; she had already seen me during a few meltdowns.

Mariah wrapped her arms around me even tighter. "Sure."

Gazing down at her, I softly said, "At nighttime we say five positive self-talks before we go to sleep. Kido, I have a new special one I will say every day and night, and it would help me if you would say it too." My daughter nodded as she watched me intently. "Here we go. Perfect health. Perfect surgery. Perfect recovery." She mouthed the words. "Are you ready? Can you say it with me?" Together we said, "Perfect health. Perfect surgery. Perfect recovery."

Sheba jumped onto the bed and Mariah giggled as she scooped up her fluffy sister. "Should I teach it to Sheba?"

"That's a good idea. I'll get your breakfast and you teach the cat while you are getting dressed for school."

After Mariah waved from the school bus, I settled down at the kitchen table with a pad of Post-it's. I began writing the mantra, peeling off the little sheets of paper as I filled them with the perfect words and sticking the notes all over the house. "Done," I said in a forceful tone.

Upstairs in my office I dialed a client. As I started to leave a voice-mail message, an onslaught of unexpected emotion welled in my throat and my words were barely distinguishable. "This is…this is D…onna… Ha…rtley. I…I'll ca…call you…ne…xt week." I burst into tears and disconnected.

I laid my head down on the desk and sobbed. *How do other people work in this state? I thought I could sound professional and talk to clients but…there are too many unknowns. My will. I'll have to check and make sure everything is in order.*

The wind rattled the office windows. I imaged the tingle of the crisp winter day and the scent of pine trees dappled by warm sun. That's where I needed to be, out there, walking off my frustrations and my plummeting mood.

Donning warm brown boots and a woven hat, shrugging into my winter parka and heavy knit gloves, I walked out the door, ready to enjoy the cold March morning. Pausing to feel the chilly air on my face, I headed toward the picture-book lake. The surreal effect of the brilliant green trees, the white trunks of aspens, and the sky radiating the vibrant richness of the day were serene. Caught up in the routine chores of each day and my discouraging cancer prognosis, I had taken the natural beauty surrounding me for granted. Stepping up my pace, I savored the mountain air and the mixture of earthy fragrances that invaded my senses. Making this decision to introduce something healthy into my day by taking a walk had given me a take-charge feeling.

Since my diagnosis on March 1st, I had been twisting like a rubber boat in a stormy sea. I existed in trepidation, helpless and vulnerable. My girlfriend, Jeanne, was right; I needed to take action. *The first step is to manage what I say and think.* My feet carried the rhythm of my thoughts. With each step I felt stronger, saying out loud, "Perfect health. Perfect surgery. Perfect recovery."

Returning to the warm, silent house, I rubbed the nip from my cheeks as I stood looking at the fridge and then gawking at my cupboards. Pulling out the trash and recycling bins, I plundered the cabinets, tossing container after container of unwholesome food. Out went the processed foods, the crackers, cookies, and anything with sugar. With each reject I hurled into the bins, I felt stronger and more powerful. Only healthy, natural food like fruits and vegetables would prepare my body for battle. I had read countless books and magazine articles and had consultations with nutritionists on the topic of eating correctly. I knew what to do, but many times I was too lazy or those not-so-good foods were tempting. Not today! I filled the trashcan again, this time from the refrigerator. I had to ready myself for surgery, mentally, physically, emotionally, and spiritually. That concept led me to believe I could do even more.

I hunkered down at the kitchen table, sipping hot tea and munching an apple, understanding this was a process, and it took me time to clarify the situation. My life called for a solid plan. I started writing.

THE PERFECT PLAN

1. **Positive Self-Talk**—*Manage the thoughts I think and say to myself. Block out negativity and fear; replace with positive words, out loud or to myself. Perfect health. Perfect surgery. Perfect recovery. When fear and doubt close in, say the words over and over, day and night, until they become natural. The mantra represents purpose…surviving this disease.*

2. **Daily Exercise**—*My body must be in the best possible physical shape when I have surgery. Exercise daily, plus spend time outdoors in the fresh air and connect with nature. I resolve to walk every day, smothered in sun block. Whenever I notice a panic attack coming on, I'll get myself outdoors and go for a walk.*

3. **Healthy Food**—*Fresh fruits and vegetables will be in my daily diet. Lots of salads, and I'll use my juicer. Beans, whole grain foods, and brown rice are a must. Eliminate caffeine and drink herbal or green tea. Fish, like salmon, high in omega-3 fatty acids, is beneficial for me before and after surgery. Snacks…walnuts and almonds. Plenty of water every day.*

4. **Tune out Negativity**—*Until surgery, no television, radio, newspapers, or internet news, because negativity will impugn my thought process. Cast off irritation and anger, do not pass judgment, and eliminate doubt. Focus on the positive.*

5. **Daily Action**—*Every day prepare my body, mind, and spirit for a successful surgery and recovery. Implement the perfect plan on a daily basis. Make it routine. I use the power of visualization, closing my eyes and seeing my body perfectly healthy.*

6. **Healing Meditation**—*Meditate consistently, morning and night. I'll create an atmosphere of peace and warmth by turning off the phone, lighting a candle, and using a blanket to keep warm. Playing music or a meditation CD helps to quiet my nerves. My relaxation begins from my toes and continues to legs, torso, arms, shoulders, and head, while inhaling though my nose and exhaling through my mouth. Next, I visualize perfect health throughout my entire body.*

7. **Supportive Friends and Family**—*Rely on friends and family to help out with my daughter. Have my friends add me to their prayers and send my positive mantra back to me.*

8. ***Alternative Medicine***—*I'll supplement my diet with vitamins and minerals and consult with my homeopathic nutritionist. I visit my chiropractor to align my body and schedule a massage to revitalize my energy.*

9. ***Team of Professionals***—*Establish a team of doctors I trust and create clear communication. I will ask lots of questions. I can empower them by taking responsibility and being a proactive patient.*

Reading through my plan, I wasn't ready to write "The End" at the bottom of the page. It was incomplete. What had I forgotten?

A sound broke through my thoughts. Hurrying to answer the ringing phone, I was hopeful it was San Francisco calling to say they had a cancellation, but it was Doctor Mandell's nurse saying he wanted to speak to me.

"Donna, when is your surgery?" the doctor asked.

"They have me booked for the end of April."

"You must get in sooner. This cancer is fast-moving. Let me know if you can schedule an earlier appointment," Doctor Mandell said before hanging up.

"I will," I said to no one on the phone. I walked back to the list I had written. *What am I missing?* My intuition was screaming at me. Whatever was missing...it was important!

Lesson Learned:
Develop a plan

Chapter Twenty-Seven
Inside a Child's Heart

On a chilly Saturday, with snow dancing lightly in the air, I dropped Mariah off to join her downhill snow ski race team at Squaw Valley and headed for the cardiologist. It had been almost two weeks since my San Francisco visit. There wasn't much time left in March.

I kissed Mariah, tucked her scarf securely around her neck, and adjusted her helmet. "Honey, I'm going to see the doctor for a short appointment. I asked your uncle and aunt to come to the race, and I'll be back to cheer you on."

She nodded, impatient to join her group. "Okay, Mommy. Bye."

I had my doctor's order for the EKG in my purse. It was only a routine procedure and I'd soon be back at Squaw Valley, since the cardiologist was only fifteen minutes down the road in Truckee. I knew I would be at the bottom of the ski hill in plenty of time to watch the kids' ski team charge the race course.

I glanced at my watch a dozen times while waiting for my results in the doctor's office. *Come on. I want to get back to my daughter.* An uncontrollable chill snaked through me as I asked the cardiologist, "You did the EKG. Then why do I need an echocardiogram? What's wrong?"

"You have a heart murmur and I am taking precautions," he stated flatly. "The echocardiogram is more detailed and will tell me what I need to know. It's important for the anesthesiologist to have this information," he said professionally.

"But I've had the murmur since I was a teenager. I had a heart catheterization at sixteen. Other doctors have heard it. I've participated in sports without any shortness of breath. Why are you concerned?"

"I want to make sure your doctors have the vital information they require before surgery. This is standard operating procedure."

"Uh-huh. Do I have a choice? Will you clear me for surgery if I don't have the echocardiogram?"

"No. You don't want to be prepped and have the anesthesiologist question your condition."

Experiencing a shift, a sudden change in heart rhythm, I felt a tingling across my chest. I shouldn't have come here alone. I would be handling this better if Teresa were here. I checked my watch. The appointment had taken more time than I expected. Mariah would be anxiously scanning the crowd for me at the ski race. At least Doug and Aunt Donna were there for her. By now, the race had already started… without me. I sighed, "Let's do it."

After the cardiologist had studied the outcome of the echocardiogram he said, "I'm going to release you for surgery and send the reports to your doctors.

Thank heavens for small favors. I am cleared for surgery. Mariah, I am on my way.

When my daughter saw me, she came running with her purple helmet bouncing up and down. "Mommy. I didn't do very well. Where were you? I was worried."

"Weren't Uncle Dougie and Aunt Donna here?"

"No, I didn't see them. They didn't come up to me after the race," she said quietly.

I gritted my teeth in an effort to keep my mouth shut, even as my frustration heightened. *Brother, why weren't you here for your niece? She's only six. She needs your support. I asked you to be at the race. Gave you the time and location. You are skiing on the mountain, so where are you? Too busy with your friends.*

My daughter watched me process my thoughts and softly said, "But I heard some other moms cheer for me."

"I am so glad they did." Tears welled in my eyes. "I am here now." Wrapping my arms around her blue parka and holding her close.

"Mommy. Don't forget, ski award ceremony is tomorrow."

"I couldn't forget that."

A huge smile crossed her face, then concern. "You look sad."

"I'm a little tired. Let's go home. I need a nap."

As we drove along the Truckee River, Mariah, in a rare moment, was subdued. I guessed she was tired. Quietly she mumbled, "I want to ask you something."

I could tell by the tone of her voice what she wanted to say was important. "Sure."

"Next year," she said looking at me, "I don't want to be on the race team. I only want to be on the ski team, not the race team." She continued as if selling me on the idea. "I know you told me you ski raced to win your father's love. I don't need to race for love. You already love me."

The wisdom of my daughter was amazing. "Mariah, you can be on the ski team. Not the race team. Fine with me."

"Thanks, Mommy," she piped in as she sat there beaming.

Oh God, I'm making a promise to my daughter for next year. Will I be here?

Lesson Learned:

Handle obstacles

Chapter Twenty-Eight
On Top of the Mountain

The temperature gauge in the car registered 20 degrees outside, but it was looking like a blue bird day—a beautiful, sunny day after a light overnight snowfall. I loved Squaw Valley on days like these. Excitement oozed out of Mariah as she chatted nonstop about the upcoming award ceremony at the top of the mountain.

We rode the tram while gazing out at miles of snow-covered peaks and Lake Tahoe in the distance. Pulling my parka tighter at my neck to keep out the chill, we headed toward the large glassed-in room of the mountain ski chalet facing the panoramic view of the valley floor. Packed with hundreds of kids and parents, the room resonated with noisy energy. It was almost more than I could handle in my current state. Grateful Mariah was in one of the younger groups, who would be awarded early on. Squaw Valley ski teams were known for turning out Olympic skiers, and this is where it all started, in the Mighty Mites program.

Even with the crush of people, my mind drifted to only one man: Mr. Wisdom, George. This was the exact room where he had bestowed on me the mysterious envelope—the package containing the gift of intuition—and it was my assignment for the next thirty days. I reflected on the events leading up to that fateful day in the Melanoma Center when I received my diagnosis. Was it my developing intuition and my trust in it that had made me go in two and a half months early for my skin check-up?

George, George, are you here? Did you know back then, before you died, that I would have to come to terms with my cancer? Were my lessons for this lifetime already cast in stone and was it up to me to see if I would survive them? Is this a spiritual cleaning for me? Is this true for everyone?

My daughter's race team group was called to the front of the room, and I was required to deal with the present. I searched the crowd for my brother and his wife, but they were a no-show. I guessed the skiing was too fantastic for them to leave the ski slopes and come in and watch their niece today—or the day before, when I had invited them to attend her race. I tried to swallow the lump of resentment in my throat and suddenly grabbed my chest with my right hand as a wave of realization washed over me; I had to live—there was no one who loved Mariah like I did.

As my daughter held up her trophy, a clear Squaw Valley mug with the ski team insignia on it in the air for me to inspect, I shouted above the racket, "Great job!" Everyone on her team received a mug. She laughed. She had done an impressive job considering she had missed so much practice while visiting Nana in Pennsylvania and other weekends when I was too sick to drive. There was no way she even placed in the top fifteen in her group. These kid skiers were diehards; snow, wind, or sleet, they showed up for practice.

"Shall we stay for the rest of the awards or can we leave now?" I asked hopefully.

Her eyes brightened as she said, "Could we go ice skating?"

I leapt at the opportunity to leave the pandemonium. "That's an idea."

She scrunched up her face. "I'm not very good at skating."

I laughed. "Hey, neither am I. When I was a kid, I skated on a pond near my house. The only way you get better at skating is to do it. Let's go!"

The vast outdoor rink was located two levels down from the main floor, where the awards ceremonies were being held, with a view that spanned for miles. Groomed and sleek, the surface sparkled like glass as the sun shone high in the sky. Only a dozen skaters or so slithered about on the ice.

After renting skates, we glided onto the ice while giggling and holding onto each other to stay on our feet, but landing on our bottoms regardless. Arms outstretched for balance and wearing a determined look on her face, Mariah skated around the rink alone.

She slipped up to me and grabbed my hand. "I can skate."

"Way to go!"

She raised her arms for a hug, and when I released her, the expression in her eyes was so serious for one so young. "Mommy, I wish I were you."

"You do? Why? You're perfect the way you are."

"Because if I were you, I'd have the boo-boo in my leg and you wouldn't be sick."

A brick of emotion struck my chest. Choking back tears I stuttered, "Ma...Mariah, I'm, I'm going to get better." I did not want her to see me cry. "I...I'm going to...skate around the rink by myself." I glided off, grappling with the words my child had just spoken. Her empathy shook me to the core. Halfway around the rink I raised my eyes up to the resplendent blue sky and prayed harder than I had ever prayed in my life. *God, I am not asking for myself... I am asking for my daughter. I signed up to raise Mariah. Please let me do my job. I promise...I promise...I won't complain about the teenage years.*

Completing the lap while swiping at tears, I neared Mariah and grabbed her hand. "I did it!"

Cheeks rosy, eyes sparkling, she shouted "Good, Mommy. You're getting stronger."

"You bet," I said with gusto. "Come on."

We skated around the pristine rink more times than I could count until she claimed, "I need a rest. My ankles hurt. I'll hang onto the railing.

You can keep skating."

Skimming the ice, more confident now, I experienced something like a wreath of peace drifting around me. I felt engulfed in a protective blanket of tranquility. Looking at Mariah, I waved, and that's when the missing piece came to me. My perfect plan wasn't perfect until I turned my destiny over to God. Step Ten of my perfect plan was to do everything I could, then let go and let God.

1. *Positive Self-Talk*

2. *Daily Exercise*

3. *Healthy Food*

4. *Tune out Negativity*

5. *Daily Action*

6. *Healing Meditation*

7. *Supportive Friends and Family*

8. *Alternative Medicine*

9. *Team of Doctors*

10. *Let Go and Let God*

Lesson Learned:
Let Go and Let God

Chapter Twenty-Nine
Make This a Magnificent Day

It was the last week in March, and I needed an appointment for surgery. Well, it was more like I pleaded every few minutes for an appointment right now. Four weeks 'til my scheduled surgery, but I wondered if I could do anything to speed up the process. It was so like me—the impatient redhead.

Since I had chosen to eat healthier, my energy level had continued to increase, and my complexion glowed. Massages and meditation helped diminish my panic attacks, and I downed my vitamins with blended protein drinks. I recalled my mentor saying, "Prepare for success. When you prepare for it, know that it is on its way." *George, are you watching? I am doing my perfect plan. I'm following the written assignment you gave me in the gift of intuition.*

Health

Good health heightens your passion and enthusiasm for life. Like a cocoon houses a beautiful butterfly, your body embodies your soul. If you abuse your body, either by poor diet, addiction, or excessive stress, you injure your soul as well. Depression, anger, and even lack of self-esteem can result.

Focus on ways to nurture your health. Drink plenty of water to rid the body of toxins and aid digestion. Avoid eating junk food that can clog the pathways to vital organs. You want to stay heart healthy. Remember what Mom said about eating an abundance of fresh fruits and vegetables? She was right. The body needs a plentiful supply of vitamins and minerals to keep your brain and organs in good working order to prevent disease.

Mark your calendar every year for your dental check-up and a doctor visit. Establish clear communication with your doctors so you are committed to a health regimen. You're worth it.

AFFIRMATION:
I am healthy in body, mind, and spirit.

There was a bone-chilling frost in the air and another winter storm was brewing as I headed to my chiropractor, Doctor Nathan Cohen, just a few blocks from my house. Living with chronic back pain and headaches since the plane crash, I thought I would take the pain to my grave, until I started treatments from the chiropractor in my small mountain town. I had traveled to the major cities to receive care from well-respected doctors, but the help I needed was right here in Tahoe City. What was that Georgeism my Mr. Wise Man used to say about a guy who left his home to travel the world in search of riches only to come home and find out one of the biggest diamonds in the world was discovered on his property? Something like that anyway, but I got the point. Especially since George had a way of repeating the parable until a light bulb went on in my head, which sometimes took a long time. With this disease there was no stalling.

"How are you feeling today?" Dr. Cohen questioned.

"I'm feeling…I'm feeling better than I did last week."

"Why don't you get on the table and let me see what story your body is telling?"

The man was complex, caring, highly educated, and had an incredible talent for understanding the workings of the body. My back pain was gone. My migraine headaches were gone. Of course, I was not disease-free, since I had cancer.

Doctor Cohen used gentle movements to adjust my back, neck, and head. "Your body is in good alignment. Are you drinking plenty of water?"

"So much I feel like I could float to San Francisco for the surgery," I confirmed with a smile.

Back home, later that morning, with a blazing fire in the hearth, I stretched out on the sofa, cuddled beneath a light blanket, and created a state of meditation. *I have an appointment at the Melanoma Center.* I thought that a dozen times. *Healing energy, go to the incision on my left thigh. My body is being cleansed of disease and toxins. I am healthy.* Deeply ensconced in my meditative state, the buzzing of the phone jarred me. *The phone again, seems like I spend most of my time answering it. Let it be good news.*

"Hello. This is Donna."

"Ms. Hartley?" a curt voice at the other end inquired.

"Yes. Speaking," I replied.

"I'm calling from UC San Francisco Melanoma Center. There is an opening for surgery this coming Thursday. We would like to schedule you at 6:00 AM Thursday morning for check-in, followed by your procedures. Can you be here on such short notice?"

Shocked by the sudden cosmic intervention, I said, "Yes. Of course I'll be there."

The woman verified my fax number and said, "I'll be sending you the pre-surgery details. You will have three procedures that day. You are an outpatient, but tell whoever is accompanying you that your release time will be late. You cannot drive. If, after you receive the information sheets, you have questions, please call the number listed on the form."

"Thank you," I said as my mind whirled with activity. "Excuse me, why did you call me?" I blurted out. I didn't think about the question, I just said it.

"Well." She paused for a moment. "I remember you standing at the patient check-out counter and saying to call if there was an opening. You were adamant."

"Oh. Yes. That was me. I'll be there. Thank you...thank you so much for scheduling me! I'm grateful."

Hanging up, I let out a whooping sound and flung a fist in the air. Sheba came running toward me. "Not to worry, kid. I'm rejoicing at the prospect of having the lousy cancer cut out of my leg. Who'da thunk, I got my early appointment, little fluff ball!" Enthusiastically I shouted, "I want to live!"

I yelled those exact words in the plane crash. I want to live! Is this the second life lesson my mentor said I would have to survive. Plane crash March 1st, 1978 and melanoma diagnosed on March 1st, 2002. I thought when George said survive, he only meant I would lose an acting contract or a boyfriend would break up with me. Never something life-threatening! There is a third lesson, he said. No, I can't think about that now. First I have to beat this cancer.

My girlfriend, Isa, insisted she would drive me to the hospital. She offered to stay and send me positive healing thoughts, but she came down with the flu and cancelled. Isa had plenty on her plate. Her husband, Brad's, symptoms of MS were advancing, and I was afraid his time on this Earth was limited. Isa promised to send me good healing vibrations from her apartment, and I accepted gladly. Gal power, yes—I was blessed with some incredible women in my life.

I asked my sister-in-law if she would take me to the hospital and she agreed. In the meantime, I kept telling myself I would be okay. Was I lying? Was I believing only what I wanted to? Had my cancer spread?

Be prepared but
expect the unexpected

The night before I left for San Francisco, I wrote out in detail who was taking care of Mariah, when and where she needed to be, and who was staying with her overnight so she could sleep in her bed with Sheba nearby. It was my girlfriends who volunteered to coordinate her school activates and dance classes.

Making sure I had food for her lunches and setting out her clothes and shoes, I choked back tears so Mariah wouldn't see me crying. My world seemed to be shifting moment by moment, and I was fearful.

After finishing up all the preparations I could, I went to my daughter's room. "Little Miss Tulip." I cleared my throat. "Please sit with me."

Noticing the serious look on my face, she snuggled up close to me on her bed. "Mommy, what is it?" she said with such innocence.

"I'm going to San Francisco for two nights. I'll be staying with Uncle Dougie and Aunt Donna and will be in the hospital also, and the doctors are going to remove this bad cancer."

"I'm scared. What will happen to me?" she said as her mouth quivered.

"Honey, Mommy is going to be fine, but if anything does happen to me, Aunt Donna and Uncle Dougie will take care of you."

"No, I want you!" Mariah screamed, grabbing me as tight as she could. The tears streamed down my face. Mariah began sobbing as Sheba came running and hopped on the bed. We cried and held each other tight until we fell asleep. Sheba snuggled in next to me.

I arrived at my brother's elegantly furnished home in Tiburon, overlooking the San Francisco Bay, moments before dusk on Wednesday night. The garden was right out of a magazine. It made me smile, since my yard in Tahoe was blanketed with a foot of snow. My sister-in-law, Aunt Donna, had gone out of her way to prepare a delicious dinner. After we cleaned up the kitchen, Aunt Donna excused herself to do some work in the study, and I asked Doug to go over the details of my will. "If anything happens to me, I want you and Aunt Donna to assume Mariah's care. We've talked about this. All the particulars are included here." I handed him a copy.

Without so much as a glance, Doug tossed the will aside. "I don't think it's necessary to discuss this right now. You'll be fine."

I gasped. *Jeez, you are stubborn, but then, so am I.* "Doug, please, you don't understand the seriousness of my situation." My shoulders shuddered. "Besides the melanoma, there's a concern about my heart. Even the most experienced anesthesiologist can't predict what might occur. We need to talk about this. I'm hoping everything goes well, but my concern is Mariah."

He seemed not to hear what I said and went right on talking. "By the way, so you're aware, the day after tomorrow we're leaving here at dawn to drive you back to Tahoe. We want to ski that day because the conditions are supposed to be ideal. My wife can drive your car, and I'll follow in mine."

"Are you serious?"

"Yes, we are leaving first thing Friday morning."

"But that's just hours after my surgery. This is a major deal."

"We're leaving early."

Down deep, I guessed he was suppressing his feelings and didn't want to deal with the idea of anything being seriously wrong with me. But another part of me wanted to scream and let him know I thought he was an inconsiderate jerk for not recognizing my fears. How could he not see the disappointment on my face? My life could be in jeopardy and my brother was concerned about snow skiing. It was the night before my big day and, now of all times, I couldn't afford any negative bunk to run loose inside of me. I made the decision not to argue, only walking away to the guest bedroom, saying nothing. I was in this alone...or was I? *There is a higher power.*

This situation is between my brother and God, and the course of my cancer is between me and God. I release my anger for the highest good. Perfect health. Perfect surgery. Perfect recovery.

The next morning, I was quiet during the drive to the hospital. "You better not park here. The lot closes at 6 PM and I won't be out by then," I softly said to my sister-in-law.

"Of course you will. That's twelve hours from now," she said tensely, her eyes scanning the lot for a parking space. She had given her word to drive me to the hospital and she was honoring that, but it was obvious she was impatient.

Is anyone listening to me? I pressed my fingers to my temples. I couldn't worry about this. Whatever happened would be my sister-in-law's lesson to learn. I had told my brother and her it was a long day with three procedures. *She will have to move the car later.*

Aunt Donna was a few steps ahead of me as we walked to the archway leading into the center, and I attempted to calm myself. It didn't work. *This is a cancer hospital. I'm having an operation. I'm scared. Run! Run away now!* When reaching the set of double doors, I stood there, I couldn't move. Finally I glanced upward. *Make this a magnificent day.* Slowly, very slowly, I walked through the doors.

After registration, my sister-in-law, myself, and my growing anxiety rode the elevator to the second floor. *This is it.* As we neared the nurse's station, anxiety hit me square in the chest. Putting one foot in front of the other took every ounce of concentration.

In the sterile bathroom, I donned a hospital gown; this one had small rosebuds on it. Suddenly I was overwhelmed. Curling into a ball on the bathroom floor, I couldn't move, paralyzed by fear. *Cancer. Cancer. I have cancer. I could die today in surgery. What about my daughter?* My mind swirled, unchecked. *Is this how my mother feels? Lying in her nursing home bed, is she overcome with anxiety? She's panicked about her mortality?*

I didn't come out of the bathroom until the nurse knocked on the door, insisting it was time. From her tone, it was clear she wasn't going away. Finally I acquiesced, opened the door, and gradually moved to the bed.

"I'll be back, and then I hook up your IV," the nurse said in her thick Russian accent. She had straight, shoulder-length brown hair, an ample figure, and a demeanor that implied she wouldn't put up with nonsense from anyone.

"An IV. I don't want an IV. I didn't know I was getting an IV," I protested. I hadn't had surgery since I was sixteen; I forgot I'd need an

IV. I didn't want this operation. I wanted to stop right now. But I needed it. I clasped my hands together under my chin with my arms tucked in tightly covering my chest.

I stared helplessly at my sister-in-law and then at the nurse. The nurse, whose name tag read Leedia, raised her eyebrows. Aunt Donna didn't say anything, but her eyes were riveted on me as if realizing this was more serious than she had anticipated.

"Why don't you call Doug and tell him what is going on," I said to Aunt Donna in a shaky voice.

"Sure..." Her voice dropped off and she quickly exited the barren surroundings.

Pungent air seemed to hang in the room. I closed my eyes. *So, it has finally arrived, my day of reckoning. I knew I'd have to face it sometime; problem is, I don't want to do it right now. Why? Why do I have this disease?*

I was facing my own mortality with this pending surgery. My father had gone in for routine cataract surgery, had a stroke, and passed on within a week. No one knows going into an operation how their body will react.

I reflected on how my mother had been so scared about dying in the nursing home that she had wanted me to die with her. She begged me to die, to kill myself so she could pass and not be scared.

During my last visit on New Year's Eve, Mariah was hysterical in the TV room, begging me to stay with her while my mother cried in the room down the hall, wanting me to be with her. After hours of torment going back and forth between them, halfway back to my mother's room I leaned against the wall and slid down, gripping my knees as I sobbed. "I can't take it any longer! I wish I were dead."

I had struggled many times during my life, contemplating whether suicide was the answer for me. There were periods where I hated what was happening in my life and thought it would be better for me and everyone else if I were not alive. What was so important about my life, anyway? I still battled my own demons, I guessed, just like my mother.

Now would my wish be fulfilled? Would I die?

Have I healed with my mother, father, and brother? Have I forgiven and accepted them? Now I have to heal with myself. I must forgive and love myself with all my faults.

The nurse bustled into the room, abruptly jarring me back to the present. I looked around, but my sister-in-law was not there. I was alone. "Time for IV," the nurse demanded. I raised my hand in protest, but she continued forcefully "You must ready for doctors. A little prick, you feel."

For my daughter, I must live. I must have this operation. I want for Mariah a life of joy and peace, one without torment. Please let me live. I choose to be her teacher.

The needle inched into my wrist. *Perfect health. Perfect surgery. Perfect recovery.*

Lesson Learned:

Deal with relationships

Chapter Thirty

Love in My Heart

The nurse returned to my hospital room. "They ready. Nuclear medicine. I take you. Your friend come? This happen now," she interjected in a commanding tone.

Aunt Donna walked back into the room. "I talked to your brother and told him this is more serious than we had considered," she said.

No kidding, I thought, gawking at her, *I've been trying to tell you and Doug this is a grave deal, but you wouldn't listen?*

The shabby ceiling filled my view as I was wheeled down the hall into the elevator and transported to the bottom floor, which had the eeriness of a dungeon.

Aunt Donna, Leedia, and I waited for an hour in the hall. Frustration laced Leedia's voice as she grumbled under her breath. "This not do. You waiting in hall. Not goot." Finally, the radiologist called my name. She rolled the gurney into a nuclear medicine chamber as my sister-in-law trailed close behind. It was set up like an x-ray room, with an entire wall of monitors. Leedia saw the alarm on my face, reached down, and patted my hand, "You all right. I back for you."

Two radiologists approached, tentative in their mannerism.

Standing beside my gurney, one briefly explained the procedure. "We will inject radioactive dye into the area of the incision on your thigh. The dye will travel to your closest lymph nodes and register on the wall monitor. The lymph nodes will be marked, so the surgeon will know which nodes to incise."

Next, I was moved from the gurney to a hard metal table, where I shivered. The tremors in my leg became more severe with each try, as the radiologist attempted to inject the needle into my thigh.

A third doctor, older than the others, shifted his gaze from monitors to me. He had an authoritative English accent. "Please stay still. The dye has to be injected into your leg," he demanded. "I must read the screens to understand where your lymph nodes are to prepare you for surgery. You understand?"

Quickly, I shifted my head to the right, stealing a glance at my sister-in-law before closing my eyes.

Calm down. Be still. Stop shaking. Keep it together. Don't unravel. Calm, be calm.

Master the moment

Suddenly, awareness was in my body. A strange sensation entered my heart. I felt my friend Isa was praying for me with such energy and love. I knew she was here with me in thought. I could actually feel her love in my heart. *The power of prayer works.* My leg steadied while tears of gratitude rolled down my cheeks. The young resident watched but said nothing as he witnessed my tears.

Love! This is love. Isa promised she would beam support and she is doing it. I could feel it. My lower body remained still as the doctors injected the needles of dye into the thigh.

Well, it is about time you relaxed. George was sending me a telepathic message. *Couldn't get through to you until you stopped your panic attack. You were blocking me.* I didn't smell his blooming cherry pipe tobacco, but

I sensed he was around me. I closed my eyes to conjure up his image. An outline of his body was approaching, like a hologram. George was communicating with me. *Relax and let the doctors do their job.* Next, I sensed the presence of my pot and pan boss from Hawaii, Chuck, who had passed on a few months ago. I missed that big hulk of a man, who had the most dynamic, outgoing personality out of anyone I had ever met. He was my coach when I sold cookware back in college; he had believed in me.

Sensing another soul was present, there was a vague image; it was the outline of my father's upper body. His spirit was looking after me, caring for me. He was sending me a mental message: He was watching over me. Healing, that is what we were doing, more healing.

There was another hazy image I could hardly make out. Comprehending the figure more than seeing it, I knew it was my grandmother—my father's mother—who had lived to be 101. As a child, I had loved making apple pies with Grammy. A peaceful sensation descended over me.

A *ping-ping, ping-ping* sound broke my reverie as I opened my eyes to see dots on the massive wall screen light up. As the pinging continued, I glanced over at my sister-in-law standing across the room. A blatant look of concern was on her face as her hand covered her mouth, and her eyes were transfixed on the enormous screen.

The resident and supervising physician marked multiple areas on my groin with a large black marker, and then they disappeared out the door. The English doctor was entering information into his computer. Leedia returned to transfer me to the gurney and wheel me to my room. In a state of shock from the all-encompassing love I had felt, I was unable to speak.

Leedia noticed my tear streaks as her eyes searched my face. "No. No. This is not goot," she said, rubbing my arm. "I fix you up." A warmed blanket was tucked around me and under my chin as the heat penetrated my body. "You must stop this. You be fine," she insisted.

I looked over at my shaken, very pale sister-in-law. The alarmed expression imprinted on her face scared me. *Did the cancer spread throughout my body?* Emotionally, I said, "Out with it, Aunt Donna. Do you know something I don't?" She didn't answer.

Lesson Learned:

Love is unconditional

Chapter Thirty-One
Divine Intervention

Two hours later, rolling into the aseptic operating room, my semi-drugged mind kept churning. *Will George show up again? This is a sterile room! Will he be smoking his pipe? Will I smell his tobacco? Will George send me a message?*

I was moved from the gurney again to a hard metal slab. As the anesthesiologist assisted me during the transfer, he leaned over and a silver zodiac sign slipped out from under his green scrubs.

"Is that a Taurus sign you're wearing?" I slurred from the medication I had been given before being brought into the operating room.

"Yes. I'm a Taurus. Do you know any?"

"As a matter of fact, I do. George."

The other anesthesiologist, who was much younger and, I assumed, training with the man wearing the zodiac said, "You need to align your body. It's not straight." After I shifted slightly, he said, "You are perfect."

My mind echoed, *Perfect. Perfect. Perfect*

Next, I counted backward. One hundred...ninety-nine...ninety-eight...ninety- seven...ninety-six...

On the outer edge of consciousness, I saw him in the distance, floating closer, coming slowly into view. Luminous eyes brimming with compassion, a smoldering pipe clutched in his hand and a face with a sagacious smile. Oh yes, I would know George anywhere. A joyful thrill surged up, flooding me with warmth, euphoria, and freedom. As I drifted toward him, I lacked the sensation of time, space, or bodily form. I knew this was unlike any dream I'd ever had. On some level, I had entered a spiritual conduit where a visual association with George was possible.

He spoke not in words, but telepathically. *Well, Donna, what do you think of the group of souls I have assembled for you?*

In a semi-circle I saw hologram-like souls suspended in the air like mobiles from the ceiling. Many of them seemed to be wearing headgear symbolizing their role: an Indian chief in a magnificent feathered headdress, a dark-skinned man with his head swathed in a brilliant white turban, a full-bearded man in a yarmulke, and doctors in surgical scrubs and caps. As the souls continued to emerge, I experienced a sensation of lightness and compassion. Was I experiencing all this in another dimension of consciousness?

I sensed George was communicating with me again. *I'm proud of your accomplishments. You ask for help for your daughter's sake, not your own.*

I don't know where I am, I thought.

George sent another message. *It is time for you to understand.*

Open your eyes, my mind screamed. *Open your eyes!* Blinding lights glared from above. I blinked several times before an image began to take shape. A golden-haired saint? An angel? I blinked again, struggling to focus. A beautiful blonde woman was standing beside me.

"Hi, Donna. I'm Amy, your attending nurse. You're in recovery and stable."

A nurse. I quickly uttered, "I was in surgery for an hour and fifteen minutes and they removed three lymph nodes. I'm sure of it."

Amy nodded and smiled as she leaned over me to adjust my IV.

My eyes fluttered as I dozed off. The next time I awoke, a man in surgical scrubs was standing nearby. "I'm the doctor who assisted your surgeon. The surgery only took an hour and fifteen minutes, and we removed three lymph nodes. We had scheduled you for a lot longer. You came through like a trooper."

"Thank you," I said softly through parched lips.

He nodded, smiled at me and Amy, who was standing next to me, and then left.

Amy raised her eyebrows as she tucked in a blanket around my legs. "That's what you said to me when you first woke up. How did you know that?"

"I knew. I just knew. There's so much rumbling around in my head... it's so fast, I can't put the images together. It's like an accelerated movie."

She shook her head incredulously. It took her a few moments before she said, "Your sister-in-law is in the waiting room. She sent in your headset and some CDs. She thought you might want to listen to them."

"I'm sleepy. Later. That was kind of her. You can listen to them." A sharp stabbing pain in my left thigh stole my breath away. "Ouch! My leg is throbbing."

"I'm going to give you something to make you more comfortable," Amy stated.

The medication went directly into my IV, and within minutes I was asleep.

When I woke again, she was sitting beside my elevated bed. "Have you been here all along?" I asked.

"I'm assigned to you. When you're in recovery, someone is with you at all times."

"Really?" I said. "I didn't know. I have a personal angel. I had visions that came during surgery. And I...I don't have that frightened feeling I had before my operation. I'm just tired."

"You rest. There's no rush to leave here," Amy said, patting my hand.

The next time I became conscious, Amy was sitting there with the earphones on, listening to one of my CDs, Wayne Dyer. *A good sign,*

I thought.

She doffed the earphones. "You're awake. How do you feel?"

I ran my tongue over my chapped lips. "Better. How long have I been here?"

"About four hours."

"That's longer than the surgery took."

A tall, gangly nurse entered the room and announced with a grin, "Whoever is waiting for you is wearing a hole in the carpet. I expect she'll be climbing the walls next."

I glanced at Amy and questioned, "Do I have to leave? I feel weak. I'm thirsty."

"No, you don't. Let's get you sitting up in a chair. I'll bring you some juice and crackers. Lean on me and take your time."

Putting weight on my left leg was painful. Slumping against Amy, I hobbled for a couple of steps. Grabbing the chair arms to balance myself, I flopped awkwardly down into the recliner. "I'm glad you're my nurse. You're very kind."

She smiled. "Let me share a little something with you. You weren't on my normal rotation. Your bright curly red hair was poking out from your surgical cap and it caught my attention. I asked the nurse who had been assigned to you and if I could rotate in and take you as my patient."

"You switched places with another nurse so you could be my nurse?" *Wonder why she did that? Is there a connection between us from another time, another reincarnation? Is she here now to assist me?* Thoughts shot through my mind unchecked.

Amy nodded as she held my wrist, pushing on it gently with two fingers to check my pulse. "Yes, I had the strangest sensation, like a current drawing me in your direction. I felt that not only could I help you, but you could help me, as well. It's really hard to explain. Am I making sense?"

I smiled. "Yes." Was this the beginning of a perfect recovery or what?

There are no accidents
Everything happens for a reason
When you understand your learning lesson
Then you can move to the next level

Gazing at her exquisite face, I said, "I appreciate you looking after me. Now, I think we'd better get my sister-in-law in here before she has a meltdown. But, Amy, please don't release me. I'm not quite ready to leave."

Aunt Donna's staccato steps echoed in the room as I was munching on my first cracker. She spoke loudly. "Oh, you look terrific. We can go home now."

Amy gingerly lifted my arm and rechecked my pulse. After a few seconds, she released my arm, winked at me, and offered, "We're not going to rush things. I have to see my patient take in some liquid and eat her crackers."

My left temple began throbbing. "Why don't you call Doug and tell him we'll be leaving soon?" I suggested.

"There's a vending machine down the hall if you want something to eat," Amy mentioned. "I need a little more time to make sure Donna is stabilized."

"Okay." Aunt Donna peeked at her watch and sighed. "I'll be back in fifteen minutes. Hopefully, you'll be ready to go. Today took much longer than I expected." She turned, briefly glanced back at me, and hurried away.

Amy threw back her head as her blonde hair bounced and she giggled. "Seems like your sister-in-law is in a hurry." My head gently nodded. "You, on the other hand, understand you can't rush recovery."

Amy took her time going over my discharge instructions, being very clear and precise, especially when it came to my pain medication. I hugged her tightly, not wanting to leave the protection of her care. Tenderly I said, "I will remember you forever."

It took an hour to arrive at my brother's house. I sat dazed in the front seat as we turned into the pitch dark driveway leading up to the house. Aunt Donna tapped the horn, rolled down the window, and shouted, "Doug, come help me bring your sister into the house!"

The front door opened and Doug appeared, coming down the walkway at a brisk pace. "Sure took a long time. All day," he grumbled. He nodded at me, but I said nothing. I was fatigued.

"Would you help me get her into the house?" His wife asked.

Wrapping one arm around Doug's shoulder, the other around Aunt Donna's, I limped my way to the guest room. Bearing any amount of weight on my leg caused excruciating pain in my groin.

After my sister-in-law helped me into my pajamas, I eased myself down onto the side of the bed, stifling the urge to yelp in anguish.

Doug walked into the room. "How do you feel?"

"Like I had a duel with a locomotive. Please, will you help lift my legs onto the bed?"

"Just lift them up."

"They cut the groin muscle on the left leg. I didn't know I wouldn't be able to walk on it or even lift it. It's painful."

Gently, he raised my legs.

"Thanks," I said, sinking back into the pillows as a wave of exhaustion came over me. "I'm going to sleep."

The digital clock read 11:03 AM. That couldn't be correct. I must be reading it wrong. We were supposed to leave first thing in the morning so my brother could ski. Feeling dizzy and disoriented, the events of the previous day came rushing back to me. *Surgery.* Using my arms for leverage, I inched my way up to a sitting position, grunting and groaning while my left leg throbbed. I called out, "Anybody home?"

Doug and Donna arrived within seconds.

"You're awake," Doug said, wearing blue jeans and a long-sleeve t-shirt. Concern clouded his face and furrowed his forehead as he took in the sight of me. I could only imagine what I must look like.

Donna's face appeared from around Doug's shoulder, a steaming cup of coffee in her hand. "How're you feeling?" she asked.

"I've had better days. I feel like I've been hog-tied and dragged for miles. Everything hurts." I peered at the clock again. "We're late leaving for Squaw Valley. I'm sorry I overslept."

"No problem," my sister-in-law said. She leaned against the bedroom door, crossing her ankles. She wore workout sweats. "Good you slept soundly." She shot Doug a look. "Your brother here had a rough night."

"You didn't sleep?"

His only reply was a shrug.

"He worried about you," his wife reported.

I stared at Doug incredulously. "You were worried? About me?"

"After Donna explained everything your operations entailed, and when I saw the condition you were in last night…" His voice trailed off. "I was concerned."

I remembered what happened the night before surgery. My brother was insistent we leave before daylight so he could ski. I just walked away. His behavior was between him and God, and the surgery was between me and God. I turned it over. *My brother admitting he is concerned, well… with my family, this is as good as it gets.* What had my mentor told me a dozen times? *"You can't teach a first grader to do twelfth grade homework. Only when a person is ready will they learn."* Healing is what my brother and I were doing, understanding each other, and healing.

Lesson Learned:

Spiritual lessons are significant

Chapter Thirty-Two

Countdown

The Easter Bunny's visit was always such a happy event in Mariah's life, and I couldn't stand to disappoint her. Right before my surgery, I arranged two baskets crammed with surprises and hid them in my closet, covered with a blanket. Tucked in the baskets were chocolate bunnies, marshmallow chicks, jelly beans, colored pens, coloring books, and a big stuffed bunny. An extra bag held plastic eggs filled with coins. The eggs were always hidden throughout the house, and Mariah's task was to find them and count the money.

The procedure had been on Thursday, Doug and his wife drove me home on Good Friday, and I had spent the entire day on Saturday in my bed recovering. Mariah would barely leave my bedroom, playing the role of the little nurse, bringing me water, hot tea, and answering phone calls from the numerous friends who checked in on me. Every hour, she would pipe up in her sweet, tiny voice, "Love you, Mommy." Even Sheba stayed curled up on my bed.

Here it was, late on Saturday night, and Mariah was fast asleep in her bed dreaming of presents from the Easter Bunny. From my bed, I glanced down the hall and could see that Mariah's bedroom door was open. No noise emanated from within. It was time to retrieve the Easter goodies hidden in my closet and hide the eggs around the house.

I stood with excruciating pain. I buckled and flopped back on the bed dramatically as Sheba grunted. "Sorry, kiddo. Didn't want to wake you," I said softly. "I didn't know my groin would continue hurt this much."

Thinking I heard a sound from my daughter's room, I froze. I waited. Nothing. Looking at the cat, I put my finger to my mouth. "Shhhhhhh... don't want to wake the little one." The cat stared at me, and if she could have, she would have rolled her eyes. "Well, you woke me," her stare seemed to say.

Finally, I limped to the closet, but the pain throbbing in my groin and leg was overwhelming. I hadn't even considered that I wouldn't be able to walk. What surprised me was that my groin, where they removed lymph nodes, hurt more than where the surgeon had made the incision on my leg to remove the cancer. Had the cancer spread to my groin? My body convulsed at that thought. Why couldn't I manage my fear? Relax and wait for the final lab reports. My concerns paralyzed me. How did other people handle situations like this? What was wrong with me? I leaned against the door to settle my nerves.

Though it was only a dozen steps from the bed to the closet, I hadn't anticipated the many trips I had to make to hide the baskets and eggs. It didn't take a NASA scientist to realize I couldn't pull off the tradition this year. Slowly and with immense effort, I dragged out the baskets filled with surprises and the bag of colored plastic Easter eggs stuffed with coins inside. The pile of Easter presents heaped outside my bedroom door was unimaginative but did the job.

The next morning, around 7:30, the sound of little feet running down the hall awoke me. I heard, "Yay, it's Easter! Easter! Easter! What did the Easter Bunny—?" Mariah stopped mid-sentence and stood in my doorway, looking down. "There is Easter stuff here? Why didn't the bunny hide my presents?"

Watching the confusion cross Mariah's face as she gazed at the pathetic spectacle, I understood the meaning of her bottom lip sticking out.

Her brows furrowed as she said in a sympathetic tone, "Poor Easter Bunny must have been very tired. He put everything in one pile."

I chimed in, "Your right, the bunny must have been very tired."

Mariah dropped to her knees as she popped open a plastic egg. She counted: "One dime, two dimes, three dimes, and one quarter. Forty-five cents." She counted the money again. "No, fifty-five cents."

Watching her, I couldn't help but feel pleased. Our little tradition had survived.

Mariah and I spent time counting change together, and then I sat back while she selected candy from her basket. *So much for breakfast.*

Sheba busied herself batting the stuffed bunny around on the bed. We were a family, though definitely not the conventional type. A Georgeism popped into my head.

You can't get to the top of the mountain
by just dreaming
You have to climb to reach the top

My mentor was right—as usual. If I wanted my life to change, I would have to do it myself.

I had stopped imagining someone coming into my life and fulfilling my dreams when I had taken the steps to adopt my daughter. It took years to find her—the child for me—and the cat, too. I had a family. No, it didn't fit the traditional mold, but I had created a life for all of us. We lived in a picturesque mountain town that looked like a postcard with its charm, friends, and a supportive community. This disease was not going to take me away from my family—I would fight it with everything I had in me.

Still, I yearned to have my stepdad here. John would have insisted everything was going to be fine and say it with such gusto that I'd believe him. I wished, too, that my mother had her full speech back so we could be honest with each other and heal our hidden wounds.

My stepmother had caused me years of pain. Had that anger festered in my body in the form of cancer and now I had to release any animosity toward her if I were to heal? My father...I sensed his spirit was with me at the hospital. He did care about me, even if he couldn't show it when he was alive. I wished we could have been closer when he was living, but as George always said, "Healing comes now, later, at death, after death, but you must heal."

I felt a sharp twinge in my groin and it spasmed down my left thigh. Mariah and Sheba needed me, and I needed them. They were my true family. I wasn't about to give up!

Lesson Learned:

Family traditions are magical

Chapter Thirty-Three
Kindred Spirits

"Doorbell, Mommy," Mariah said, busy arranging her jelly beans by color.

"Please look out the window and see who it is."

She jumped to her feet, plastic eggs and jelly beans flying in all directions, and ran down the hallway, I heard a moment of silence, and then she came running back.

"It's Nancy."

I nodded for Mariah to go to the front door and unlock it.

Mariah walked back into my bedroom tugging on Nancy's hand. "Nurse Nancy, what would I do without you?" I said as I sat up straighter in bed and smiled at my freckle-faced friend. A brown bag was in the other hand not being held by Mariah's. Mariah quickly chimed in. "Did Sydney come with you? Is she still in the car?"

Nancy looked down at Mariah and smoothed her wild hair. "Sorry, Mariah, she's home with her brother. They are supposed to be cleaning their rooms."

"Wow, that sounds like a good idea. Don't you think so, Mariah?

Cleaning your stuff?" I winked at Nancy.

Mariah stuck out her lower lip. "No, today is Easter Bunny Day."

Nancy chuckled. "I'm here to check your mother's bandage." She set the small brown bag she was carrying down on the bed.

"Ugh. I'm going to my room."

"My Easter gift to you is to get those dressings changed," Nancy commented, smiling, as Mariah ran down the hall.

"That's not exactly what I had in mind when it comes to an Easter present, but really, thanks for doing this—especially on a holiday." As I had been many times before, I was touched by Nancy's loyal and committed friendship.

Ignoring my comment, Nancy opened her bag and sized up my thigh, studying it for a few seconds before yanking at the tape holding the bandage in place.

"Yikes!"

"Gotta do it quick. Hurts less."

"Yeah right. Seems to me it hurt plenty."

I hadn't yet seen the surgeon's handiwork. When Nancy pulled back the bandage, I peeked at the incision and my felt stomach contract. *Whoa.* Tracks of black thread tattooed my thigh, and the wound itself looked red and puffy. The incision was way more invasive than I expected, and my stomach flip-flopped. Nurse Nancy skillfully applied a fresh bandage and then went to work on the dressing where my lymph nodes had been removed from my groin.

Glancing at me and noting my look of worry, Nancy said, "Donna, I've seen plenty of doctors' work in my day job, and I can tell you this looks pretty good." She gently poked my left groin area.

"I'm not one of your patients at the hospital. I'm your friend."

Nancy snickered "This is coming along fine. You'll be good as new in no time."

It looked pretty gross to me. What did I know about recovery? I could present a speech before hundreds of people and not blink an eye, but blood was definitely not my thing.

After reassuring me again that I was healing "perfectly," Nancy promised she'd be back the next day and left in a whirlwind of energy. *That perfect word again.*

The next time I awoke, I heard, "Meal delivery is here."

"Hey, Cathee, I'm in the bedroom. Come on in."

My energetic girlfriend with a radiant smile entered the room carrying a tray of food. "Happy Easter!" she chirped enthusiastically. "And surprise—the bunko girls and your friends have created a food chain for dinners and I am first on the list. It goes on for a month." Cathee grinned. "Not only are the bunko girls great at rolling the dice, but they're fabulous cooks, too."

"For thirty days? Are you serious?" I sat up in bed and adjusted my pajama top.

Handing me a piece of paper, she continued, "Here's the list; the bunko gals signed up first. Tomorrow is Catherine, then Ginny, Lynda, Mary, Cindy, and Katie. After that comes your friends: Angela, Nancy, and, well, you can read the names. At the bottom are some other friends who will pick up your mail and drive Mariah to and from school."

Looking at the list, then gawking at Cathee, I said, "Really? Y...you did this for me?" My eyes welled with tears.

"No, I didn't do anything. It was all your friends who called me and volunteered. They know we are close, so I put the list together."

"Cathee, you are incredible. A good friend." I fought back tears, and my voice cracked. "Sometimes, I...I don't feel like I fit in or belong..."

Cathee reached down and put a comforting hand on my foot, which was covered by a warm blanket. "You're there for us," she said. "The community. The schools. You raise money. You don't take no for an answer when something needs to be done."

I looked away, suddenly abashed. "I feel like I'm pushy."

"You're a doer. Now, let me fix you and Mariah a plate of real food, instead of candy," she said as she eyed the empty wrappers on my bed.

"Where is Mariah anyway?"

"In her room playing, or maybe ripping it apart. Hope she's cleaning up some." I rolled my eyes to show my doubt. "Mariah wouldn't even leave my bedroom yesterday, but I think she senses I am doing better today."

For ten days, I had my routine down to a pattern of sleep and talk to my girlfriends when they dropped off meals or took Mariah to school or drove her home. The excitement of the day was having dinner with Mariah. In the middle of all this, my daughter landed a part in a play and had mandatory practices. She had tried out for the part and got it the day I was in the hospital. I was thrilled, since it kept her mind busy studying her few lines instead of worrying about me. I considered it good karma.

My phone rang nonstop with my pals checking up on me, and the outpouring of my friends was almost overwhelming at times. John also called every once in a while, checking in to give me moral support. I truly felt cared for. Joan came into my office two days a week to handle the details and follow up on phone calls, but I asked her not to schedule any speeches for me. I didn't know my future. She sat at the bottom of my bed after she finished work, filled me in on what was happening, but in reality she was lifting my spirits.

Whenever the phone rang, my heart jumped, hoping and also dreading that it was the hospital calling with my post-operative results.

At night, when I was alone and Mariah was in her bed, I cried. I cried for the love I felt from my friends. But I also cried because when it was dark and still in the house, my fears accelerated and I worried about why it was taking the hospital lab so long to release my reports to me. Was it more serious than I suspected? Had the cancer traveled throughout my body?

The surgeon's office booked an appointment for a follow-up meeting on Monday. They wanted me to come in person so the doctor could inspect my leg. *What about the cancer?*

The night before going back to the hospital for my lab report, I woke with a start, conscious of warm air on my face. "Mariah, what's wrong?" I asked my daughter, who was leaning over me.

"I was checking to make sure you were breathing."

Quickly, I sat up and turned on the light. The clock read 1:14 AM. "It's the middle of the night."

"I know," Mariah spoke in a whimper, "I love you. Tomorrow you go to the doctor. I'm scared."

"I'm a little scared myself." Noticing her serious look and the sadness in her eyes, I asked, "Do you want to sleep in my bed with Sheba and me?"

"Yeah! Wait one minute," she bellowed as she ran down the hall with her nightgown flowing. She burst back into my room with her pink blanket and six stuffed animals.

Looking at the cat, I warned. "Move over."

Mariah arranged her stuffed animals in a line and went down the row saying good night to each one while wishing them sweet dreams. Sheba looked at the stuffed animals, then at me. I only shrugged. The cat curled up on a corner of my pillow and Mariah took the other side. I smiled as I squeezed in the middle. I had taken the mundane for granted. I wouldn't anymore.

A few hours later, the sound of the massive county snow plow roaring down the road at 5 AM was not a good sign. Minutes later, I heard a smaller plow roar up my driveway going back and forth. Cautiously, I eased myself from the bed and hobbled to the window. There were five inches of snow blanketing the street and big white flakes still coming down. Who would believe it was April?

Mariah and Sheba were still sleeping when the phone rang. "Donna, you need to get on the road before Donner Pass closes. It could be a squalling whiteout up top," Cathee said. "Drop Mariah off at my house. We're all set for her. Don't worry. She'll be fine while you're gone."

Johanna called next. "Ready to rock and roll to San Francisco? My husband woke me when he got ready for work. I'm dressed and heading out in a few minutes. Checked on the pass and it's still open. Not to be concerned, we'll make your appointment."

"Should I worry more about the drive or the doctor's report?" I asked as I poured a cup of tea and inched my way back to my bathroom to dry my hair.

"Neither. I'm on the way."

Johanna possessed an inner strength; she was a mountain gal, and in her spare time she went snow skiing, biking, hiking, or was out on the lake. Intense and up-front, with a husband plus two boys around Mariah's age, she buzzed from one activity to another, centering her life on family and community. Johanna was my secret weapon. If the surgeon's news was bad, I could count on her strength.

Driving to San Francisco took over five hours due to the blizzard conditions. Once we cleared the mountain pass and the closer we traveled to the Melanoma Center, the more apprehensive I became until my body started jerking and I began sobbing. Johanna pulled the car off to the side of the highway and parked. Turning and wrapping her arms around me. "It is going to be fine."

My sobs grew louder. "That...that's what everyone is saying, but what if it isn't? What about Mariah? Who will raise her? My brother is too busy with his life to give her the love and attention she needs." The rush of weeping continued as Johanna held me, but slowly, her warmth and inner strength helped settle my nerves. My thoughts drifted to my mother and how scared she must feel without her drinking friends around to support her. They had abandoned her—everyone but her husband. I was blessed, truly blessed, to have so many friends.

Later, supported by Johanna, we passed through the entrance to the Melanoma Center. She shouldered a large canvas tote overflowing with my books and CDs, all gifts I had packed for the nursing staff on the second floor.

When we reached the sterile nurse's station, Leedia, my Russian nurse, glanced from behind the counter, her normally stoic face breaking into a smile. "You look goot."

Smiling back, I said, "I'm on my way to the surgeon to find out my results."

"You very well."

"Leedia, thank you for being thoughtful when I was...well, not the best patient. I've brought some gifts; my books and CDs for you and the nursing staff."

Johanna began removing the contents of the tote and setting them on the counter.

Another nurse I remembered seeing on the floor the day of my surgery moved to the counter and held up a CD. *"Fire Up Your Life!* Yes, I could use some of this."

Leedia walked out from behind the nurse's station and hugged me. "You nice person. Health to you."

Happy for the moment, I forgot about the roulette wheel down the hall waiting to spin my destiny.

Trussed up in another undignified gown, this one with tiny blue dots, I was seated on the exam table, waiting for Dr. Allen, the surgeon who had performed my operation, to appear. Johanna attempted to make small talk but gave up after a while. I wasn't good company with concern stabbing at me. The walls seemed to close in around me, and my future shrunk down to mere minutes.

Abruptly, an intense, large man with mahogany-colored skin charged into the room. With only a nod at Johanna and me, he proceeded to remove the bandages. Though his absence of bedside manner threw me as it had the first day I met him, I only prayed he had been brilliant in the operating room.

He peered down at the stitches. "Yes. This is good." Prodding and poking. "Healing nicely."

"Doctor," I finally squeaked, "the melanoma, what about the cancer?"

"You're fine." He fumbled around in his coat pocket. "I have that report here." He pulled out a folded sheet of paper and handed it to me.

Unfolding the paper, I gazed down at the biopsy report. *Lymph node #1, no tumor. Lymph node #2, no tumor. Lymph node #3, no tumor. Skin, left thigh, no residual melanoma.* I read the rest of the words, not understanding some of the medical terminology, until I read the last line. *Negative for melanoma.* I read it again. I read it one more time. *Negative for melanoma.*

Caught deep in my own contemplation, I understood I would not need any radical treatment. I did not have melanoma in my body. The surgeon couldn't find any cancer, yet the mole on my left thigh had been biopsied twice and both reports came back with stage III. My eyes moistened. Did something happen at the top of Squaw Valley when I gave up my fears and turned it over to God?

The paper slid from my grip as my hands flew to my mouth as I softly mumbled, "Thank you, God."

Lesson Learned:

Community is your support group

Chapter Thirty-Four

Another Chapter Closed

Outside, the snow from yesterday's storm was melting and the trees were richly embellished with the buds of spring. Brilliant red tulips and yellow daffodils poked up from the ground, pushing the snow away and heralding a colorful flourish of blooms that signified a new beginning.

I was now in the recuperating phase and had moved to the overstuffed chair in the living room. After Mariah was picked up for school and I gave her a half-dozen kisses, I snuggled under a blanket to meditate. As Mr. Wise Man used to tell me, "Life is simple; it is man who complicates it." I was on this planet another day to learn more lessons. Why did I always have the underlying feeling that I was working off my karma for three lifetimes?

Midmorning, the phone rang, and before picking it up, I marveled how this device was able to keep the communication lines open between me and so many people. Glad I didn't live in the old western days. Hmm, a thought flashed across my mind, maybe I did.

"Hi, this is Donna."

"Glad you're sounding like you have more energy," my brother said.

"Amazing how great I feel knowing I don't have melanoma. Now

I just have to remember it's all about healing." I paused, attempting to formulate my next thought. "It all boils down to learning lessons."

"What was yours?"

"Interesting—good question." Running my hand over the armchair fabric, I reflected for a moment. "Live more, stop worrying, have fun, appreciate the small things, say 'I love you,' and heal." I then ran my fingers through my hair and scratched my head. "Yeah, and don't build up anger. Let it go...let it go right through me so I don't end up disease-ridden."

"Wow," Doug said with surprise in his voice.

"This disease was scary for lots of reasons. It humbled me. It showed me how precious life is. So many times I took life for granted instead of appreciating every moment."

"Uh huh," he said.

"I'm not saying life is a piece of cake, because I've certainly had some challenges. I just wish I would have gone right a few more times instead of cutting my own path. I had to live the lessons to comprehend them." I shifted my body in the oversized chair and stretched out my legs on the ottoman to relieve some of the pressure on my groin.

"The ordeal we went through with Mother and then Father, whew— I'll never choose that again. But the healing was wonderful. I want to feel better about all my relationships, including ours."

Doug stated enthusiastically on the other end of the line, "You'll feel even better when I give you the news."

"Really? What? "

"We finalized Mexico today."

"Does that mean the condo is ours?

"It does."

"No more hassles with the builder?"

"He signed off."

"The stepmother?"

"It's ours."

"You're sure." I jumped to my feet with excitement. "Oh, ouch, my leg!"

"Are you all right?"

"Yes," I grunted and gently lowered myself down on the chair. "I just stood up too fast—wasn't thinking. I can't believe it's finally ours. This news is worth the pain." Then, self-doubt clouded my joy. "It really is ours, right? No glitches, no mistakes?"

"Absolutely. I received the documents by mail. I'm gazing at two copies as we speak, one in Spanish and the other in English."

Adjusting my shoulders into the back of the cushy chair, I let out a sigh of relief. "I can hear the sound of waves washing up on the beach already."

"I'm glad you're better. Now all we need is for the Stepmother's house to sell and we can close the books on everything," Doug said with a hint of frustration.

"We've been at this for years trying to get this deal closed. I'm afraid it's going to take a miracle." *But miracles happen.*

Lesson Learned:

Restore your life

Chapter Thirty-Five

A Week to Remember

Healing my body was taking time, but every day I felt a little better. A girlfriend stopped by and dropped off a wonderful old hand-carved cane so I could hobble around the house easier.

After Mariah headed out to school each day, my routine was fairly simple. I would take out my juicer and blend up fresh fruit, and then I'd meditate, write in my journal, drink water, read a positive book, schedule a massage, and take a nap. Work and money would come later—at least, that's what I wanted to believe. Besides, this is what I would consider a marvelous week: Monday, no cancer. Tuesday, we finalized the Mexican papers and the condo belonged to Doug and me. Now it was Friday and I was just plain happy to be on planet Earth.

The phone chimed its musical ring as I lifted myself with the support of the sturdy cane and limped toward the phone. Leaning against the wall I said, "Hi, this is Donna."

"Your probate case is over. The house in Nevada sold," Janet said with satisfaction in her voice. "The judge has approved the documents so you and Doug will be paid the percentage you are due."

"It's over?"

"Yes."

I lowered my head. *A perfect ending to a perfect week.*

"Donna? Are you there?"

I raised my head, grinning into the phone. "Oh, yes, I am here."

"Good, I will have the papers sent over next week to sign."

"Thank you...thank you again for everything," I said as I hung up, sensing the tension release from my shoulders. Almost every time my attorney had called in the past, it was to inform me of another obstacle that had to be overcome. Not today. This was sheer joy. I would say it was spiritual rebate time—everything had worked out better than I could have hoped or imagined.

George, are you around? Are you listening? Please be listening, because your student is learning. Three wonderful events happened this week; no cancer, the Mexico condo has clear title, and finally the war ended. When the time is right, change happens.

There are no accidents
everything happens for a reason
Once you understand your learning lessons
then you can move to the next level

My mentor's words were simple, yet it took me years to appreciate the wisdom behind them.

Every action produces a force of energy
Negative action generates negative energy
Positive action generates positive energy

Mr. Miracle Man, your sage knowledge has guided me through some challenging times.

> *Heal now*
> *Heal later*
> *Heal at death*
> *Heal after death*
> *You must heal*

George, sweet George, if you were sitting around my dining room table smoking your blasted pipe, you would probably ask in your slow Oklahoma drawl with your eyes squinting like you were deep in contemplation, "Well, did you get it?"

I'd chuckle and say, "Thank heavens I didn't know it was going to be this hard or I wouldn't have signed up for these tough lessons."

You'd let out a belly laugh and insist, "You are only given what you can handle."

Of course I would disagree, and you would merely say, "Count your blessings."

My blessings...hmmm, my blessings. I went through hell, some turbulent years, but I came out the other side with some mighty powerful healing. I begged for over twenty years to heal with my mother, father, and brother, and that healing came in ways I never could have anticipated. The blessing I never envisioned was the healing that took place in my body, mind, and spirit—learning to forgive and accept myself for who I am today with all my faults.

Mariah is the reason I am alive. She gave me the will to fight my disease, to be a survivor when at times I was almost paralyzed by anxiety. My daughter and fluffy Sheba loved me unconditionally. I know now that the ingredient needed for healing is unconditional love.

George, right now you would take your pipe out of your mouth, tap it on the table a half dozen times, and in a low, slow tone deliver your sage wisdom. "Never said healing was easy, but we all must find healing within ourselves and within our relationships before we can move on with our lives. Otherwise, we're stuck making the same choices—some of them quite possibly harmful to our health and happiness instead of helping us to grow spiritually."

When he was still alive, George confirmed that in the plane crash, I was given enlightenment so that I would speak, write, and help people help themselves. When I was about to burn to death in the accident, the thought that permeated my brain was I'd have a daughter late in life who would be a leader. George acknowledged this. He'd said that I had three life lessons and that I had to develop and trust my intuition to learn them. "Surviving them is your choice," I could hear him saying now. "Do you want to fulfill the assignment bestowed on you during the plane accident?"

I was suddenly shocked out of my imaginary conversation with my mentor and back into the present. The plane crash had been lesson one, surviving melanoma was lesson two. I still had one more lesson! I whispered aloud, "Please, let it not be life-threatening like the last two."

In the distance I heard a dog bark, and I could feel that the reverberation was one of fear. Was this an indication of what was to come?

Lesson Learned:

Healing is a process

Lessons Learned

1. Healing starts with you
2. Learn from your past
3. Trust your intuition
4. Act on your intuition
5. Healing begins with little steps
6. Ask for guidance
7. Have the faith of a child
8. Let magic happen
9. Forgiveness is powerful
10. Focus on a positive outcome
11. Be open to unexpected help
12. Healing happens when the time is right
13. Truth and integrity prevail
14. Perseverance triumphs
15. Survive the journey
16. For the highest good
17. Believe in your dreams
18. Honest relationships are essential
19. Power of spiritual wisdom
20. Celebrate each day
21. Face your destiny
22. Friendship is caring

23. Live in the moment
24. Have inner strength
25. Be proactive with your health
26. Develop a plan
27. Handle obstacles
28. Let Go and Let God
29. Deal with relationships
30. Love is unconditional
31. Spiritual lessons are significant
32. Family traditions are magical
33. Community is your support group
34. Restore your life
35. Healing is a process

Your Ten-Step Perfect Plan To Health

Your body has done countless things for you. Have you said thank you? Do you appreciate your health? Have you honored your body, mind, and spirit by being kind to yourself and others and by staying healthy?

If you could use some help infusing more spiritual, emotional, and physical well-being in your life (and who doesn't?), here is your ten-step perfect plan for your health. It takes action and follow-through on your part, but know that you are worth it!

Whether your goal is to maintain your health or you are dealing with a disease, you play a major role. Start by taking a few of the healthy steps in the perfect plan and implement them. First, feed yourself with positive self-talk. This is easy to do. Focus on and say affirming words to yourself and out loud 'til they become natural and you believe them.

Next, become aware of the food you eat and make healthier choices by adding more vegetables and fruits to your diet. Write down what you eat each day — you could be surprised to find out you eat more than you think. Also what type of foods make up your eating pattern, it might not be the energy food that serves your body. This is a great way to check on your food intake.

Meditate in a quiet room with soft music or a guided meditation CD. It takes only 10 to 20 minutes. If you want to develop your intuition, be calmer in your decision making, and how you react in a crisis, meditation is the path. This is the best way to release stress.

To kick-start your exercise program, set out your sneakers and workout clothes the night before so you almost have to trip over them in the morning and you are reminded it is time to get your body moving.

Follow the plan below and activate all ten steps. It takes time and commitment, but the results are positive. Claim your health, combat disease, and experience the rewards of feeling better. If you forget or stop the plan, don't beat yourself up, but start again the next day.

I am not a doctor, I am a survivor and so are you!

PERFECT PLAN

1. **Positive Self-Talk**—Manage the thoughts you think and say to yourself. Block out negativity and fear and replace them with positive words you say out loud or to yourself. Perfect health. Perfect surgery. Perfect recovery. Or, Perfect health. Perfect energy. Perfect alignment. Or Perfect_____. Perfect _____ Perfect_____. When fear and doubt close in, say the words over and over, day and night, until they become natural. The mantra represents purpose: surviving your health concerns.

2. **Daily Exercise**—Your body must be in the best possible physical shape to stay healthy. Exercise daily or a minimum of three times a week. Also, spend time outdoors in the fresh air and connect with nature. Resolve to walk, smothered in sun block. Whenever you notice you are depressed or feel a panic attack coming on, get outdoors and walk—burn off that stress.

3. **Healthy Food**—Fresh fruits and vegetables are crucial to a daily diet. Eat lots of salads and invest in a juicer. Beans, whole grain

foods, and brown rice are a must. Eliminate caffeine and drink herbal or green tea. Fish (like salmon) is high in omega-3 fatty acids and is beneficial for a healthy body—especially before and after surgery. For snacks, eat walnuts and almonds. Make sure you drink plenty of water every day.

4. **Tune out Negativity**—If you are going through a health crisis, no television, radio, newspapers, or internet news, because negativity will impede your thought process. Cast off irritation and anger, do not pass judgment, and eliminate doubt. Focus on the positive.

5. **Daily Action**—Every day, prepare your body, mind, and spirit for a successful, disease-free experience. If surgery and recovery are required, then believe in and see a healthy outcome. Implement the perfect plan on a daily basis. Make it routine. Use visualization by closing your eyes and picturing your body restored to perfect health.

6. **Healing Meditation**—Meditate consistently. Create an atmosphere of peace and warmth by turning off the phone, lighting a candle, and using a blanket to keep warm. Playing music or a meditation CD helps to quiet the nerves. Relaxation begins from the toes and continues to the legs, torso, arms, shoulders, and head while you inhale though your nose and exhale through your mouth.

7. **Supportive Friends and Family**—Rely on friends and family to help out. Don't be afraid to ask—you might be surprised at the love and support you receive. Have your friends add you to their prayers and send your positive mantra of perfect health back to you. When people think about you, they should only focus on the perfect words that create the perfect outcome.

8. **Alternative Medicine**—Supplement your diet with vitamins and minerals by consulting with a homeopathic nutritionist. Visiting a chiropractor or an acupuncturist is an excellent way to relieve pain and align your body. A massage will revitalize your energy.

9. **Team of Professionals**—Establish a medical staff and team of doctors you can trust and have clear communication with. Ask lots of questions. The more knowledge you have, the better informed you will be about your health. Empower yourself and your medical staff by being a responsible and proactive patient.

10. **Let Go and Let God**—Turn it over to a higher source.